THE BOOK OF
HAPPISBURGH

Mary Trett and Richard Hoggett

with the Happisburgh Heritage Group

HALSGROVE

Part of the Village of
19 HAPPISBURGH

Village life in Happisburgh in 1953, drawn by Mary Trett.

First published in Great Britain in 2011

British Library Cataloguing-in-Publication Data
A CIP record for this title is available from the British Library

ISBN 978 0 85704 097 8

HALSGROVE
Halsgrove House,
Ryelands Business Park,
Bagley Road, Wellington, Somerset TA21 9PZ
Tel: 01823 653777   Fax: 01823 216796
email: sales@halsgrove.com

Part of the Halsgrove group of companies.
Information on all Halsgrove titles is available at: www.halsgrove.com

Printed and bound in the UK by the MPG Books Group

*Frontispiece image: Fishing boats pulled up from the
beach in front of the first coastguards' houses, c.1890.*

CONTENTS

Acknowledgements 7

Chapter 1: **Living on the Edge** 9
    The Village Sign 10
    Sources of Information 10
    Coastal Erosion 11

Chapter 2: **The Earliest Humans** 20
    Handaxes on the Beach 20
    The Cromer Forest Bed 24
    The Ancient Human Occupation of Britain Project 25

Chapter 3: **Prehistoric and Roman Happisburgh** 29
    Archaeological Evidence 29
    Prehistoric Flints 30
    Mesolithic 30
    Neolithic 30
    Bronze Age 32
    Iron Age and Roman Periods 36

Chapter 4: **Anglo-Saxon and Medieval Happisburgh** 41
    Early Anglo-Saxon 41
    Middle and Late Saxon 44
    The Origins of Happisburgh 44
    Domesday Happisburgh 46
    Wymondham Abbey 49

Chapter 5: **Happisburgh Church and Clergy** 53
    The Building 53
    The Bells 57
    The Vicars of Happisburgh 59
    Reverend Theophilus Rice (1724–75) 59
    Reverend James Slater (1816–95) 60
    Ernest Watling (1926–2002) 67

Chapter 6: **Happisburgh in the 16th–18th Centuries** 68
    Churchwardens 68
    The Constable 69
    John Gerard 70
    The Parish Register 71
    The Middletons and the Chamberlins 74
    Village Tradesmen 75
    Reverend James Farrer 76
    Jonathan Chaloner 76
    Original Sources 76

Chapter 7: **The Cruel Sea** 77
    HMS Peggy 78
    HMS Invincible 79
    Hunter 83
    HMS Ranger 83
    Young England 83
    The Beachmen 83
    The Coastguard 85
    The Rocket Brigade 86
    The Happisburgh Lifeboats 88

Chapter 8:   **Happisburgh's Lighthouses** 95

Chapter 9:   Education in Happisburgh 105
              Miss Elizabeth 'Bessy' Thompson (1876–1958) 109
              Extracts from the School Logbooks 110
              The School Today 111

Chapter 10:   **Agriculture in Happisburgh** 112
              The Farming Year 112
              Agricultural Workers 116
              Three Happisburgh Farmers 117
              Happisburgh Mill 118
              Livestock 120
              John Millar (1852–1935) 120
              The Hasbro Herd of Gloucester Cattle 121

Chapter 11:   **Happisburgh in the 19th–20th Centuries** 122
              The Hill House 126
              Shopping in Happisburgh 128
              Mrs Selina (Nellie) Grimmer (1865–1948) and her family......132
              Jonathan Balls, the Village Poisoner (1768–1845) 133
              Wilfred Bion 134
              Village Events 135
              The Happisburgh Line 138
              St Mary's 140
              Henry Moore and Barbara Hepworth 142
              A Dissenting Voice 143

Chapter 12:   **Happisburgh at War** 144
              World War Two 146
              Happisburgh 4.7-Inch Coastal Battery 148
              Happisburgh Chain Home Low radar station 149
              The Home Guard and Civil Defence 150
              Extracts from the Civil Defence Logbook 150
              Extracts from the Joel family diaries 151
              German War Graves 152
              Peacetime 153

Afterword: **Looking Forward** 154

Bibliography 156

Subscribers 158

Acknowledgements

This book owes a great debt to the enthusiasm and commitment shown by the residents of Happisburgh, who have lent photographs, given valuable information and reminiscences, and shown much interest in the village. Particular thanks are due to the founder members of the Happisburgh Heritage Group: Jim Whiteside, Chris and Christine Dye, Carol Palfrey, Nikki Piggott, Vini Pereira, Colin Young and Helena Ancell. Thanks are also due to Sylvia Andrews, Mike Chambers, Cedric Cox, Tom Dobson, Shirley Everett, Murray and Julia Ferguson, Colin and Barbara Forder, Jennifer Grier, Tim Grimmer, Bob and Margaret Henderson, Gilbert and Joan Larter, Malcolm Kerby, Carole and Neville Lee, John Marshall, Rodney and Mary Mason, Clive and Sue Stockton, John and Barbara Weddall and Edna Whitwood. The authors are particularly grateful for the written contributions supplied by Tim Pestell, Patrick Tubby, Alison Yardy, Julia Ferguson, Sally Hardy and James Albone.

Thanks are due to the Coastal Change Pathfinder team at North Norfolk District Council, particularly Rob Goodliffe, Rob Young, Peter Frew and Marti Tipper. At the Norfolk Historic Environment Service, thanks are due to David Robertson, David Gurney, Alice Cattermole, Ken Hamilton, Alison Yardy, Sophie Tremlett, Sarah Horlock, Nellie Bales, James Albone, Erica Darch and freelance illustrator Jason Gibbons. At Halsgrove, the support and enthusiasm of Simon Butler and Denise Lyons have been greatly appreciated.

Permission to reproduce images has been provided by: Addison Publications Ltd, the Ancient Human Occupation of Britain project, Archant, the Bridgeman Art Library, Christie's, Tony Hall, the Henry Moore Foundation, Christopher Joel, the Norfolk Historic Environment Service, Mike Page, the Norfolk Museums and Archaeology Service, Vini Pereira, Jo Sharplin, Neil Storey and Trinity House. Thanks are also due to those who have helped to source documents or photographs: Clive Coward (Tate Gallery), Rebecca Matthews (Griffon Area Partnership), the staff of the Norfolk Record Office, Jonathan Draper (Norfolk Sound Archive), Clare Everitt (Picture Norfolk) and Eric Shanes.

Alice Cattermole deserves special thanks for reading and commenting on drafts of the text, her attention to detail and her patience as this book inched ever closer to completion.

Finally, a great debt is owed to all of those Happisburgh residents, past and present, who have seen fit to write letters, take photographs, record interviews and report any discoveries made on the beach and in the fields. This book could not have been written without them.

Chapter 1

Living on the Edge

The north-east Norfolk village of Happisburgh is famous – perhaps infamous – for the severe coastal erosion which has affected the cliffs on which it stands. Indeed, this erosion is all that many people know about Happisburgh, a sentiment which is captured perfectly by the humorous postcard recently produced by *Eastern Daily Press* cartoonist Tony Hall showing a family desperately trying to prevent their beach hut from falling over the cliff. Yet there is much more to Happisburgh than eroding cliffs,

and this book aims to redress the balance by presenting an overview of Happisburgh's rich and varied heritage, which literally spans the full range of human history, from the earliest traces of human occupation up to the present day. Along the way a number of local characters are introduced, some of whom have played significant roles in the history of the village, others of whom have added a splash of colour to everyday life. As a picturesque and highly desirable coastal location, the village has attracted

This postcard by cartoonist Tony Hall humorously captures the popular perception of Norfolk's eroding coast (Artwork by Tony Hall; image © J. Salmon Ltd, Sevenoaks, Kent)

more than its fair share of famous visitors, among them artists, actors, writers and poets, and accounts of their visits are also included here.

The Village Sign

Many of the stories of the history of Happisburgh told here are depicted in the village sign, which stands on the crossroads in the centre of the village, near to the church. On the right-hand side of the sign stands Edric the Dane, the holder of Happisburgh manor at the time of the Domesday Survey in 1086. After his expulsion, the estate eventually passed into the hands of Roger Bigod, whose daughter Maud stands on the left-hand side of the scene. Maud married William d'Aubigny, who was given the Happisburgh estate as a part of her dowry, and d'Aubigny was ultimately responsible for Happisburgh's coming into the hands of the

The village sign, depicting several scenes from the history of the village.

monks of Wymondham abbey in the 12th century. In the centre of the village sign scene stands the Reverend Thomas Lloyd, the 18th-century vicar of Happisburgh who believed that the reason why so few children were being baptised was because their parents could not afford to give a party afterwards. Lloyd therefore offered to provide the post-ceremony entertainment himself and on Whit Sunday 1793 baptised 170 people.

Below the village name can be seen the twin towers of the parish's most significant landmarks – the church and the lighthouse – between which is placed an heraldic shield bearing an ear of wheat, a symbol of the agriculture which has supported the settlement since its earliest days. At the bottom of the sign is a carving of one of the original Happisburgh lifeboats, another powerful reminder of the long and sometimes dangerous relationship which the settlement of Happisburgh and its inhabitants have had with the sea.

Sources of Information

The material presented here draws on a rich array of personal reminiscences, collections of postcards and photographs, as well as historical and archaeological sources and archives. Old photographs and postcards are an invaluable resource to anyone wishing to research local history, and a large number of images held by present and former residents of Happisburgh have been made available to the authors in the course of putting together this book. Many families have collections of photographs which they think may be of no interest to anyone else, but this is seldom the case, and it is important to encourage those know to make notes of the names of the people and events pictured!

Large numbers of historic documents relating to Happisburgh are held by the Norfolk Record Office, located on the County Hall site outside Norwich, where they are free to be consulted by anyone interested in finding out more about the parish. Many of these documents have been used to write this book, although there are still an enormous number of documents which remain to be studied, lots of them containing fascinating insights into the history of Happisburgh. The Norfolk Record Office also hosts the Norfolk Sound Archive, an archive of oral history recordings, which already includes a few Happisburgh recordings and which will hopefully be receiving more in the near future. In this book, references which begin with the abbreviation NRO refer to material held by the Norfolk Record Office. Further information about the Norfolk Record Office and the Norfolk Sound Archive, including a searchable catalogue, can be found online at http://nrocat.norfolk.gov.uk

The Norfolk Historic Environment Record (NHER) is maintained by the County Council's Historic Environment Service and comprises a digital database, computerised map and vast paper archive. It contains details of all of the known archaeological sites and monuments in the county, as well as Norfolk's architecturally significant buildings and records of the results of over 30 years of amateur metal-detecting. References which begin with the abbreviation NHER refer to entries in the Historic Environment Record and can be read about in more detail via the online version of the Historic Environment Record, the *Norfolk Heritage Explorer* at http://www.heritage.norfolk.gov.uk.

The Historic Environment Service also curates the Norfolk Air Photo Library, a collection of over 85,000 aerial photographs of the county dating from 1895 to the present day. These photographs offer an incredibly detailed record of the county from the air, including many archaeological and historical sites which are only able to be seen and understood properly from the air. The library is open to the public by appointment and further details can again be found on the Norfolk Heritage Explorer website.

Coastal Erosion

Happisburgh has lost land to the sea throughout the centuries. The rate of erosion has been erratic – at times large areas have disappeared overnight, and at others the cliff has remained virtually the same for some years. The rapid rate of erosion on this particular stretch of coast is due to a combination of the soft and unconsolidated nature of the geological material which makes up the cliffs (deposited by glaciers approximately 478–424,000 years ago), the groundwater which percolates through this material and, most significantly, the angle at which the waves hit the beach. The north-easterly prevailing wind drives waves straight onto the shore, dragging away beach material and moving it to the west and south through the action of longshore drift.

Dramatic erosion in this part of the county is not a new phenomenon. Numerous settlements

An aerial photograph of Happisburgh taken in June 2007, showing the dramatic effects of the erosion to the south of the village where the sea defences have failed (© Mike Page)

recorded in the Domesday Book in 1086 have subsequently been eroded, some of them comparatively early in the medieval period, surviving only as names in the documentary sources. One of the most well-known local examples is the Domesday settlement of Shipden, the precursor to modern Cromer, which had ceased to be mentioned in historic records by about 1500, by which time it had presumably been eroded. Closer to Happisburgh, there is now no trace of the Domesday settlement of Whimpwell, thought to have been a fishing village on the seaward side of Happisburgh. Documentary sources record that by 1183 only one field remained in Whimpwell, but the name lives on the Happisburgh place-names of Whimpwell Green and Whimpwell Street (Darby 1971, 103). More dramatic evidence of the destructive force of the sea was seen at Eccles, the successful fishing village to the south of Happisburgh, which was effectively destroyed in one night during the violent storm of 4 January 1604, leaving only the church tower standing (Storey 2009, 102–03). The church tower survived until the 1890s, becoming the subject of many paintings and early photographs, before it finally succumbed, and the buried remains of the settlement have been periodically exposed by the scouring action of the sea ever since (Pestell 1993).

Happisburgh, too, has been particularly badly affected by erosion. In his *Norfolk Directory* of 1836, William White wrote of Happisburgh that 'the church is a lofty pile, with a fine embattled tower, 112 feet high, standing on an elevated point of land, within a short distance of the sea-cliff, which, rising perpendicularly, and having an under stratum of sand and gravel, is so continually wasted by the agitation of tides and storms, that it is calculated the church will be engulfed in the ocean before the close of the ensuing century, the sea having encroached upwards of 170 yards during the last 60 years' (White 1836, 320). That same year, William Hewitt, a Stalham surgeon, suggested that breakwaters should be constructed parallel with the cliffs. He believed that these would cause sand to accumulate on the foreshore. He noted

that those set at right angles to the cliff caused sand to build up on one side only. His idea was based on observations of the wreck of the Revenue cutter *Hunter*, where a sandbank had formed between the wreck and the shore, and stretched almost to Walcott. A violent storm shifted the vessel and the bank disappeared. Hewitt also suggested sinking hulks of old ships a short distance from the shore. Some landowners acted upon his advice, but the wrecks became a hazard to shipping and were later removed.

Other examples of the dramatic rate of the erosion are offered by parish records from 1845 which indicate that a twelve-acre field at Happisburgh was drilled with wheat, but that a north-westerly gale raged all night and by the next morning the field had disappeared. Similarly, in 1855, the farmhouse and a large barn at Doggett's Farm were lost to the sea. So great were local concerns that in the late 19th century, the local author Ernest Suffling wrote: 'The modern village is gradually being swept away; scarcely a winter passes but a few yards of the sand along the coast are swallowed by the furious north-west gales which prevail. Fields which, during my own recollection, contained several acres, have either entirely vanished, or have dwindled to mere patches.' He continued, 'During a severe gale in January, 1895, I witnessed the effect of the heavy sea upon the soft clay cliffs; the succeeding waves simply *melted* the cliffs so rapidly that the water was of a deep warm brown colour … the old buildings now stand nodding upon the brink of the cliffs, but still occupied by persons who must tremble in their beds on a stormy night for fear that they may be swept away before dawn' (Suffling 1897, 170–1).

On Saturday 31 January 1953, a strong north-westerly of over 110 miles per hour caused the worst disaster since the flood in 1287. The sea claimed the lives of 76 Norfolk residents and flooded thousands of homes. An exceptionally high evening tide whipped up by the gale was two hours earlier than predicted. It surged down the east coast, smashing sea defences and flooding low-lying land. A bungalow at

This photograph from the early 20th century shows the dilapidated coastguards' houses teetering perilously close to the top of the cliffs. Such scenes have been all too typical in Happisburgh for many generations.

Happisburgh, which at teatime on Saturday stood 15 feet away from the cliff, was hanging over the cliff edge on Sunday morning. By 8:00pm the surge reached Sea Palling and burst through the sand dunes, carrying away four houses, a café, a general store and a bakery. Families clung desperately to roof tops until rescued by Stalham Fire Brigade in a commandeered dingy. Twenty or more were saved, but seven died, including a mother and her three children.

The cliffs at Happisburgh suffered severely from erosion throughout the 1950s. Falls of cliff were frequent, even exposing the foundations of the Happisburgh's redundant second lighthouse (of which more later), and in 1958 access to the beach at Town Gap became impossible meaning that no boats could be launched. In response to the

A rather grainy photograph of Happisburgh from the air, showing the stormy seas experienced during the 1953 floods and the damage which they caused. This photograph was taken by the Ministry of Defence during Operation Floodlight, an aerial assessment of the impact of the floods. Photographs from this survey are held by the Norfolk Air Photo Library (© Crown Copyright 1953/MoD: TG33/TG3831/A. Reproduced with the permission of Her Majesty's Stationery Office)

The effects of the 1953 floods on the cliffs at Happisburgh. The building on the clifftop was the boathouse of the first Happisburgh lifeboat, demolished a few years after this photograph was taken. (Image courtesy of Norfolk County Council Library and Information Service)

The construction of the first set of sea defences at Happisburgh in 1958/59.

A postcard view looking north along Happisburgh beach, showing off the newly constructed sea defences and groynes.

An aerial view of the Beach Road area from the north-east taken on 25 May 1970. The timber sea defences and zig-zag groynes can be seen on the beach, as can the double row of posts belonging to a second set of sea defences tucked in against the base of the cliff. (© Norfolk County Council)

An aerial view of Happisburgh from the north-east taken on 22 July 1970. Note the hexagonal pillbox on the beach in the foreground, which appears to have recently tumbled from the clifftop. (© Norfolk County Council)

threat posed by this erosion, the first steel and wood sea defences were built at Happisburgh in 1958/59 and were later extended. As a result of their construction, the rate of erosion decreased, any loss of land being due mainly to surface water causing falls of cliff, and the clifftops came to be densely populated with caravans and bungalows.

At various times during the following decades portions of the revetment were destroyed and repairs were carried out on numerous occasions, but even these defences did not always succeeded in preventing the erosion, although they did slow its progress considerably. The sea defences began to fail in the 1980s and the erosion became particularly bad again in the 1990s, as breaches went unrepaired while attempts were made to find a solution to the problem. On 21 February 1993, ferocious waves caused havoc along the coastline and at Happisburgh a large portion of cliff was swept away causing a bay to begin forming to

the south of the village and resulting in the loss of farmland. Worse was to come, when on 19 February 1996 during a prolonged gale and snowstorm the sea defences were breached and a bungalow perilously close to the clifftop eventually succumbed to the sea. Having broken through, the sea began to enlarge the new bay to the south of the village, which continued to grow over the ensuing decade. A comparison of two photographs taken by aerial photographer Mike Page in October 1996 and May 2006 give a stark indication of how much this short stretch of coastline has changed in just a decade.

In 1999, a public meeting was called in the village for residents to discuss what course of action should be taken to address the problem of the failed sea defences. This meeting had originally been intended to be held in the Church Rooms, but when hundreds of people started turning up the venue had to be rapidly changed to the church. This meeting saw the establishment of the Coastal Concern Action Group,

This aerial photograph from 1996 dramatically illustrates the devastating effects of the sea on the clifftop dwellings at Happisburgh. (© Norfolk County Council, photographed by D.A. Edwards: TG3830/AB/HFH5)

This photograph and the next graphically illustrate the significant changes which have occurred in Happisburgh since the sea defences were breached in the mid-1990s. This photograph was taken in October 1996, and clearly shows the beginnings of the bay to the south of the village. (© Mike Page)

An aerial view of Happisburgh taken in May 2006, illustrating the extent of the bay to the south of the village and the losses to the north of Beach Road, including the collapse of the lifeboat ramp which necessitated its move to Cart Gap in 2003. (© Mike Page)

In August 2003, some 500 residents of Happisburgh formed the letters SOS on the clifftop to draw attention to their plight. (© Mike Page)

which, under its chairman Malcolm Kerby, has campaigned tirelessly for social justice for the residents of Happisburgh. Another public meeting was held in Happisburgh in January 2003, this time attracting over 600 people, and in order to draw attention to the village's plight in August 2003 a Coastal Concern Action Group publicity stunt saw hundreds of villagers spell out the letters SOS in the field opposite Beach Road. The resulting aerial photograph was picked up by a number of different media outlets.

During the early years of the 21st century, central government attempted to explore a number of different options to help with Happisburgh's predicament, but none was without objectors and, somewhat ironically, the rapidly changing physical environment meant that the technical specifications of each suggested solution changed rapidly. In December 2004, a draft Shoreline Management Plan was put out for consultation, the plan stating that rather than holding the line, controlled retreat was the only affordable and sustainable way to manage the erosion in Happisburgh and elsewhere on the Norfolk coast.

This announcement was met with anger and dismay by local residents, who felt abandoned by central government, and the campaigning continued. A public fund-raising campaign to pay for additional sea defences was mounted, and in 2007 an additional 1,000 tonnes of rock were added to the 4,000 tonnes which North Norfolk District Council had already placed on the beach at the end of Beach Road in 2002.

Then, in 2009, after several years of discussions with affected parties, the Department for Environment, Food and Rural Affairs (Defra) invited local authorities to apply for money from an £11-million funded Coastal Change Pathfinder Programme. The Pathfinder Programme was intended to be an 18-month 'road test' for local authorities to explore ways of helping coastal communities plan and adapt to coastal change. North Norfolk District Council (NNDC) were successful in securing £3 million to trial its projects between December 2009 to April 2011.

Although elements of the North Norfolk Pathfinder Project focussed elsewhere within North Norfolk, the majority of its initiatives focussed on Happisburgh, where it brought a new hope and vitality to the community. A number of different approaches to solving the village's problems were trialled during the Pathfinder Project, perhaps the most high-profile element being the scheme by which North Norfolk District Council offered to buy the properties of those residents whose houses were most at threat of erosion, enabling them to move house and clearing the way for the demolition of those properties to create a buffer of open land along the clifftop. In addition to demolition, the clifftop enhancement incorporated the provision of a new car park, public conveniences, beach access, clifftop paths and information panels. Enhancements also extended to the beach, with the removal of debris from the damaged and broken sea defences making the beaches a considerably safer and more pleasant environment.

One final element of the North Norfolk Pathfinder was a Coastal Heritage Project, hosted by Norfolk County Council's Historic

Some of the broken sea defences at Happisburgh, as photographed by Vini Pereira. He and many other local photographers and artists take great inspiration from the sea defences. (© Vini Pereira)

Environment Service. The project was established with the intention of encouraging Happisburgh's community to study and record their heritage through the provision of advice, training and equipment. This element of the Pathfinder project saw the establishment of the Happisburgh Heritage Group and has resulted in the publication of this book.

"Well basically, Lionel was pruning the buddleja when I shouted the good news up the garden, and unfortunately he – er – jumped for joy."

The announcement of a compensation scheme for clifftop homeowners as a part of the North Norfolk Pathfinder Project as marked by Eastern Daily Press *cartoonist Tony Hall. (© Tony Hall)*

Chapter 2

The Earliest Humans

The Palaeolithic period encompasses a vast amount of time, from as early as 950,000 BC until 10,000 BC, and includes several periods of glaciation during which the region was sporadically occupied (Wymer 2005a). Flint tools are one of very few classes of archaeological artefact which survive from this period and a great many worked flints and waste flakes have been discovered in and around Happisburgh, where the geological layers which contain them lie not far below the surface of the beach and are periodically exposed. Among these flint artefacts are some of the earliest man-made objects so far discovered in Great Britain, and indeed northern Europe, rendering Happisburgh beach internationally significant in archaeological terms.

Handaxes on the Beach

One of the most characteristic Palaeolithic tools is the handaxe, which was knapped (flaked) from flint and used for a wide range of cutting, chopping and butchery tasks. These axes come in a range of shapes, but tend to be oval, relatively thick and broadly symmetrical on both faces. As the name suggests, the tool was held in the hands and used directly to strike or cut objects, unlike later stone axes which were hafted onto wooden handles. Flint handaxes of this kind have frequently been discovered on the beaches of north-east Norfolk and the distribution of these discoveries comprises a broad arc ranging from the Runtons in the north to Pakefield in northern Suffolk, but there is a particular concentration of discoveries on the stretch of coast from Happisburgh to Horsey (Robins, Wymer and Parfitt 2009).

A relatively large number of Palaeolithic handaxes have been recorded from Happisburgh, although in many cases the circumstances of their discoveries and, crucially, the details of exactly where they were found often remain unknown. This is particularly the case with some of the older discoveries, but given that all of the handaxes for which the discovery locations are known have been found on the beach, it seems likely that these other artefacts were also found on the beach. Several of these handaxes have been discovered by members of the public who have reported their finds to the Norfolk Museums and Archaeology Service or to the Historic Environment Service, while many of the more recent discoveries have been made during archaeological investigations undertaken on the beach. In many cases the reported artefacts have been examined and sketched by an expert with the results being added to the Norfolk Historic Environment Record. For the purposes of this book, all of the sketches made of these handaxes have been inked up by archaeological illustrator Jason Gibbons so that, for the first time, all of the known handaxes from Happisburgh for which drawings exist can be published together. In certain cases it has been possible to borrow the artefacts themselves, and we are grateful to the finders for allowing us to do this.

Among the earliest recorded discoveries is a handaxe which was discovered in Happisburgh, presumably on the beach, by a member of the Sussex Archaeological Society in 1930 (NHER 12509). This artefact is on loan to Norwich Castle Museum, and the illustration published here is the first time it has been drawn

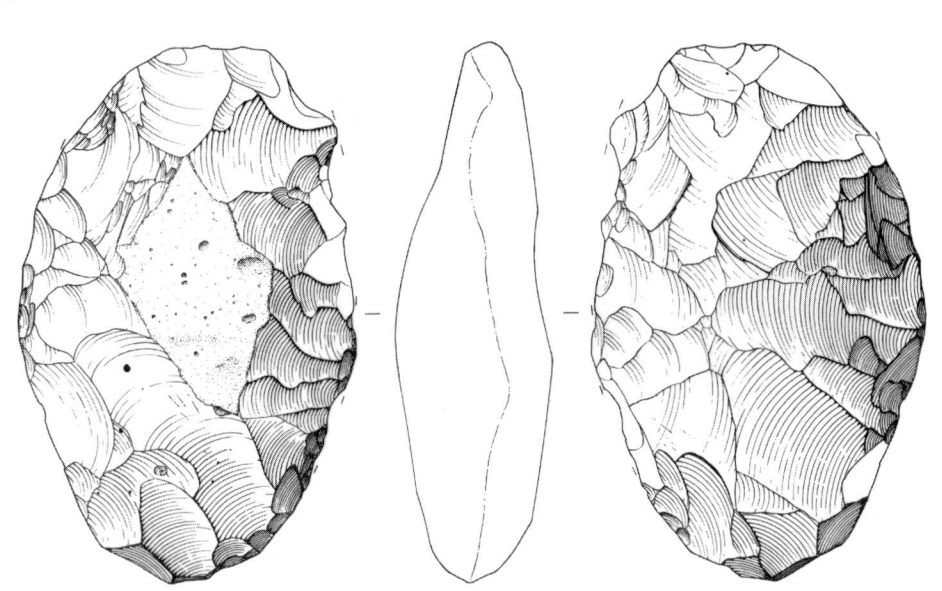

not to scale: actual height approx 14cm

Above: *Palaeolithic handaxe discovered by a member of the Sussex Archaeological Society in 1930. (NHER 12509; NWHCM: L1977.2; drawn by Jason Gibbons)*

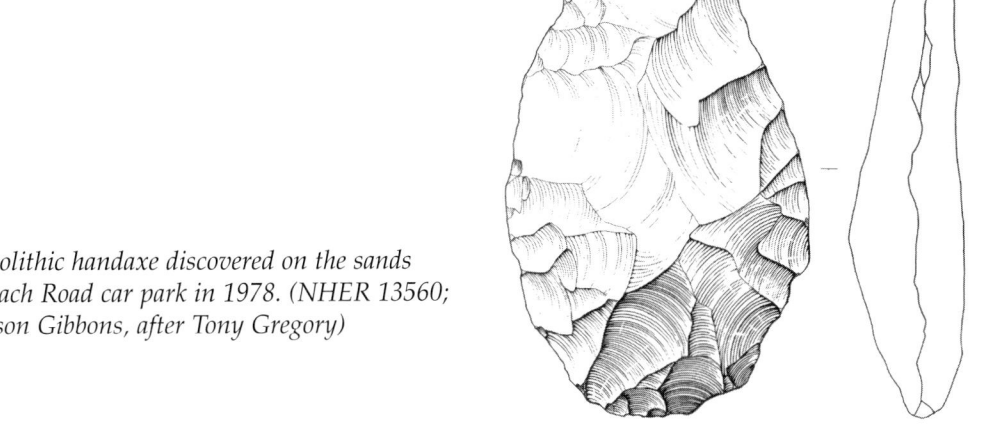

Right: *Palaeolithic handaxe discovered on the sands below the Beach Road car park in 1978. (NHER 13560; drawn by Jason Gibbons, after Tony Gregory)*

not to scale: actual height approx 13.5cm

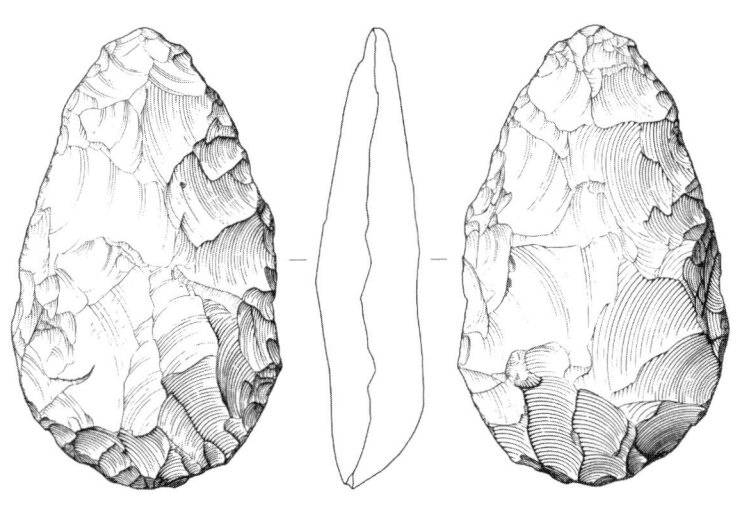

Palaeolithic handaxe discovered on the beach between Happisburgh and Eccles in 1991. (NHER 55740; drawn by Jason Gibbons)

not to scale: actual height approx 12cm

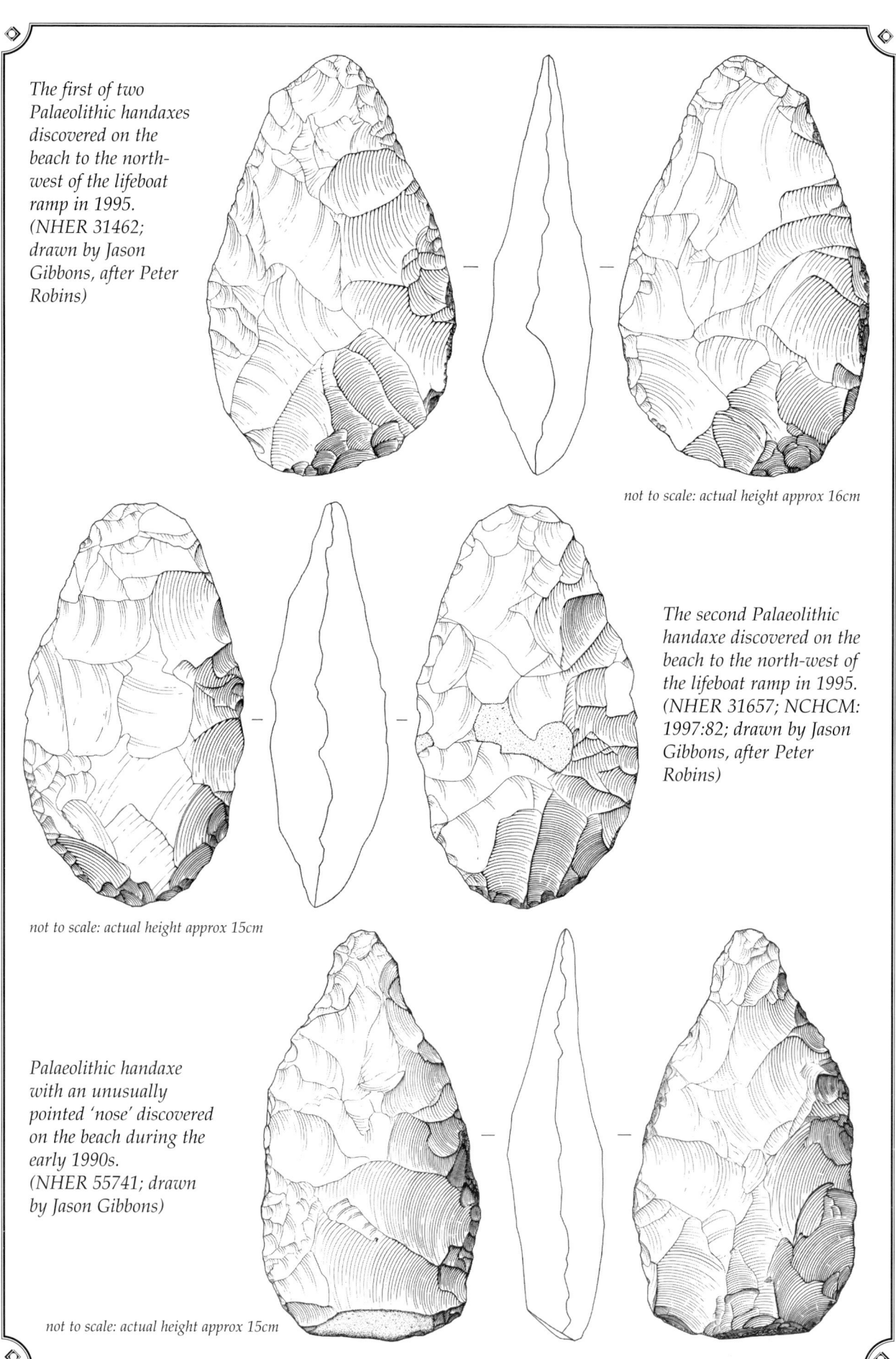

The first of two Palaeolithic handaxes discovered on the beach to the north-west of the lifeboat ramp in 1995. (NHER 31462; drawn by Jason Gibbons, after Peter Robins)

not to scale: actual height approx 16cm

The second Palaeolithic handaxe discovered on the beach to the north-west of the lifeboat ramp in 1995. (NHER 31657; NCHCM: 1997:82; drawn by Jason Gibbons, after Peter Robins)

not to scale: actual height approx 15cm

Palaeolithic handaxe with an unusually pointed 'nose' discovered on the beach during the early 1990s. (NHER 55741; drawn by Jason Gibbons)

not to scale: actual height approx 15cm

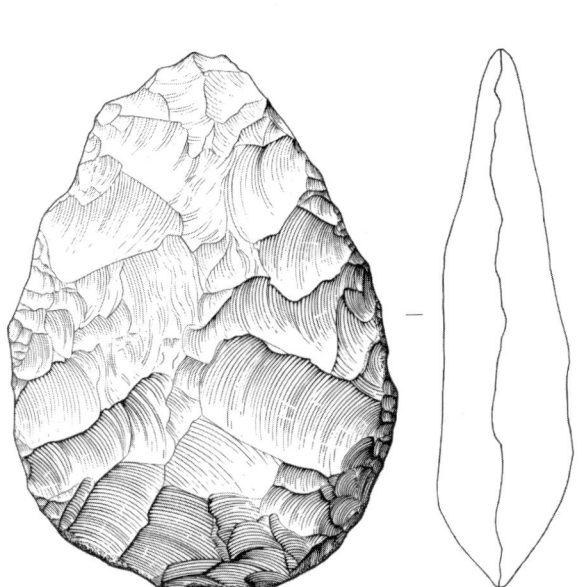

not to scale: actual height approx 14cm

Palaeolithic handaxe discovered near to the foot of the cliffs to the north of the caravan park in October 2001. (NHER 36532; drawn by Jason Gibbons, after J.J. Wymer)

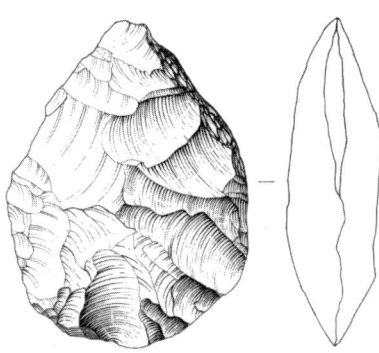

not to scale: actual height approx 9cm

Palaeolithic handaxe discovered near to the foot of the cliffs to the north of the caravan park in December 2001. (NHER 36532; drawn by Jason Gibbons, after Peter Robins)

Palaeolithic handaxe, probably made from a single large flint flake, discovered on the beach in 2008 and reported in 2011 as a result of publicity surrounding the Coastal Heritage Project. (NHER 55742; drawn by Jason Gibbons)

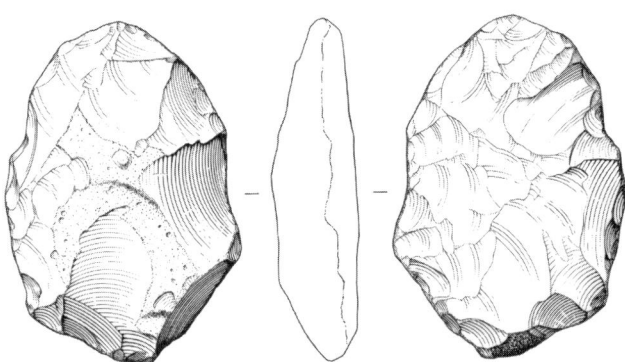

not to scale: actual height approx 9cm

Palaeolithic handaxe discovered on the beach immediately to the north of Cart Gap in 2009. Note the small flakes taken off the edge to keep the axe sharp. (NHER 52939; drawn by Jason Gibbons, after Peter Robins)

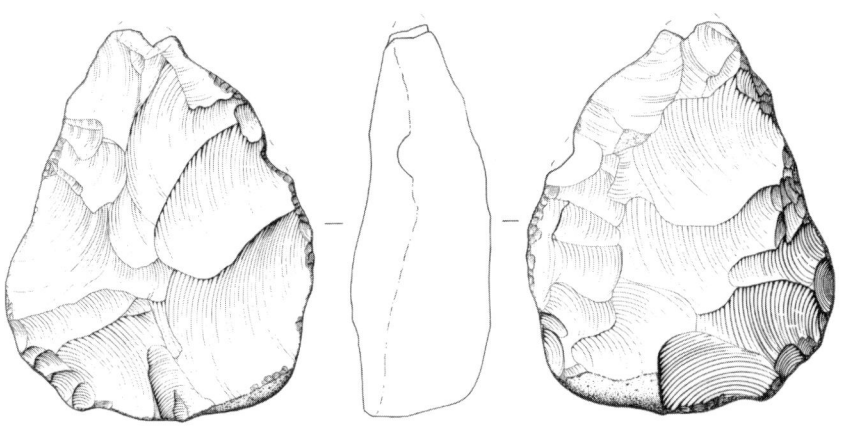

not to scale: actual height approx 11cm

(NWHCM: L1977.2). This example and many of the other handaxes which have been discovered show signs of having been rolled heavily by the sea, indicating that they have been eroded from their original archaeological context and have been moved freely around the beach for some time. However, a few of the axes show little or no sign of having been rolled and still have relatively sharp edges, suggesting that they have only recently been exposed and perhaps do not lie very far from their original locations. Tellingly, almost all of the unrolled handaxe discoveries from Happisburgh have been made in or around the vicinity of the old lifeboat ramp at the end of Beach Road, indicating that significant archaeological deposits may lie in that area.

The Cromer Forest Bed
One question which had long puzzled researchers was whether the handaxes which were being discovered on the north-eastern coast of the county, and in Happisburgh in particular, were eroding from the cliffs and falling onto the beaches or whether they were being eroded from beneath the beach itself. This is a particularly significant question, because under the sand at Happisburgh lies a part of the Cromer Forest Bed, which was laid down between 1.8 million years ago and 500,000 years ago (Wymer and Robins 2006; Preece and Parfitt 2008). The Cromer Forest Bed deposits have long been recognised as a rich source of fossils, and as long ago as October 1659, noted local antiquarian Sir Thomas Browne wrote to Sir William Dugdale describing the head and bones of a very large fish to be seen at Happisburgh, which had recently been revealed by a fall of cliff. The fossils of elephants, their teeth in particular, have been frequently discovered, many of them doubtless derived from the Cromer Forest Bed. In 1821, fishermen dredging for oysters in the newly discovered bed off Happisburgh brought up quantities of bones and, reportedly, some 100 elephant molars. Five years later, an elephant's tusk 9½ feet long was dredged up. Further specimens have been exposed on the beach, especially when a south-easterly wind veers suddenly to the north or north-west, sweeping away the overlying sand. A breakthrough came in the late 1990s, when Simon Parfitt was working through collections of fossils in the Natural History Museum which had been collected from the Cromer Forest Bed by Alfred Slavin in the late 19th century. In doing so, he discovered a previously unrecognised cut-marked – and therefore butchered – bison bone from Happisburgh. This was immensely significant, for this butchered bone provided the first evidence of human activity from the Cromer Forest Bed (Preece and Parfitt 2008, 61).

In early 2000, the Quaternary Research Association (QRA), an organisation devoted to researching the history of the Ice Age, undertook a visit to the eastern region which included a stop at Happisburgh to view its cliffs and where Simon Parfitt was able to draw attention to his discovery. As fortune would have it, later on that same tour the QRA visited Pakefield in Suffolk where the party discovered a worked flint flake in freshly exposed Cromer Forest Bed deposit – the first such artefact to have been found *in situ* (Preece and Parfitt 2008, 61). Subsequent searching and a follow-up excavations revealed further *in situ* flints at Pakefield, proving conclusively that exceptionally early human artefacts were to be found in the Cromer Forest Bed (Parfitt 2008).

A few weeks after the QRA visit to Happisburgh, in March 2000, local man Mike Chambers was walking his dog along Happisburgh beach, near to the ruins of the Low Light, when he discovered a worked flint handaxe firmly embedded in a muddy deposit which had only recently been exposed by erosion. In an interview recorded in February 2005 and available via the Sound Archive at the Norfolk Record Office (NRO AUD5/1/1, MD1), he recalled:

'That's all that was sticking out of the ground, about an eighth of an inch just on one side, but it's as near to a straight line as you can possibly get, and straight lines, as far as I'm concerned, are unusual in nature, so it was some-

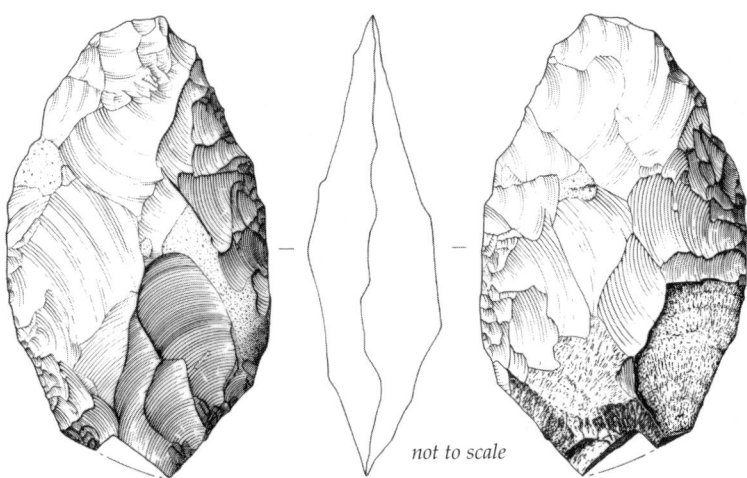

The Palaeolithic 'Happisburgh handaxe' discovered by Mike Chambers in 2000, actual height 12cm. (NHER 35385; drawn by Jason Gibbons, after John Wymer)

not to scale

Front and back photographs of the Palaeolithic handaxe discovered by Mike Chambers in 2000, shown half actual size. (© Norfolk Museums and Archaeology Service)

thing to look for. … Then, as I dug it out you could begin to see what was coming... was quite difficult to get it out of the clay, without an implement you'd never have got it out. The clay was compacted all the way around it.'

Mike Chambers had discovered another flint handaxe, but unlike the other examples, this handaxe was in mint condition, except for an ancient break at its butt end, and was found firmly embedded in the remains of the Cromer Forest Bed. Having retrieved the handaxe he took it to Cromer Museum, and from there was referred to Norwich Castle Museum, where the handaxe was examined by Peter Robins and John Wymer. Mike Chambers again:

'Until I spoke to the museum, I didn't realise how important it was. When I got I touch, they sent me this little chart which showed a cliff, all the way down from the soil at the top to the sand layers and everything else, and said "Please tell us where you found the handaxe in the cliff". When I wrote to them and told them that I didn't find it in the cliff, it's another ten, maybe fifteen foot down, that's when the interest really started. It didn't come out of the cliff, it came out of very low tide, and the area where it was is inaccessible any other time, so it was a long way down.'

On the basis of its location and the circumstances of its discovery, a date of 700,000 years old was suggested for the handaxe, immediately making it one of the oldest human artefacts to have been discovered in Great Britain at that time. Word of the discovery spread quickly among the research community and a flurry of activity ensued in and around Happisburgh as the hunt for further evidence of early human occupation began in earnest. Local archaeologists continued to monitor the area of the discovery when it was exposed at low tide and recovered a number of other flint flakes.

The Ancient Human Occupation of Britain Project

Fortunately, the Happisburgh and Pakefield discoveries coincided with the start of the Leverhulme-funded Ancient Human Occupation of Britain (AHOB) project, charged with investigating the timing, landscapes and environments of human occupation in Britain across the Palaeolithic, and their attention soon turned to Happisburgh (Stringer 2006, 7–9).

In 2001, a mechanical excavator was used to trace the course of the Cromer Forest Bed back to the base of the cliff to confirm its relationship with the cliff's more recent geological deposits, yet more worked flints were revealed in the process and the deposit from which the original handaxe was dug was identified as the floodplain deposits of a large river (Wymer and Robins 2006, 463–6).

In May 2004, a three-week archaeological excavation was undertaken at the spot at which Mike Chambers had discovered his handaxe – the site being referred to as 'Happisburgh Site 1' by AHOB (NHER 35385). Excavation conditions were difficult, as the site lay below the tide line and was regularly inundated, but this additional archaeological work revealed further evidence for early human occupation in the form of worked flint flakes discovered in association with cut-marked and butchered animal bones. The environmental evidence recovered was also particularly well preserved, and

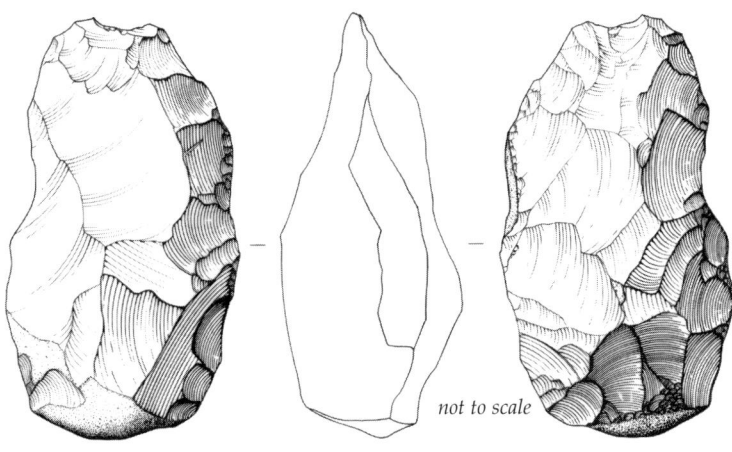

not to scale

Palaeolithic handaxe discovered embedded in the base of the cliff by Simon Parfitt and John Wymer in 2004, height approx 11cm. (NHER 55744; drawn by Jason Gibbons, after John Wymer)

comprised abundant remains of beetles, pollen and plant fossils, as well as the fossilised bones of a range of fish, amphibians and mammals, including rodents, deer, rhinoceroses and a species of giant beaver. Wood charcoal was also discovered, but it was not possible to ascertain whether this was a product of man-made fires or of naturally occurring woodland fires (Ashton *et al.* 2008).

While these excavations were underway, Simon Parfitt and John Wymer took the opportunity to explore the beach and the cliffs further, in search of other exposed Palaeolithic deposits. At the foot of the cliffs near to the site of the former lifeboat ramp they discovered an outcrop of gravel which had yet another handaxe firmly embedded in it, although this

example showed some signs of having been damaged by geological movements during its time in the ground (NHER 55744). The site of this discovery came to be known as Happisburgh Site 2, and further fieldwork around the site revealed other worked flint flakes in the same location (Wymer and Robins 2006, 467).

In June 2005, the AHOB team began to try and put these isolated discoveries into their wider context by excavating a series of exploratory trenches every 50–100m for a distance of 2.5km along the foot of the cliffs at Happisburgh. This work identified the vicinity of the metal stairs down to the beach and the upturned Second World War pillbox – now referred to as Happisburgh Site 3 – as having the greatest potential for revealing further early human occupation evidence and environmental data, and so further archaeological excavations began in earnest.

AHOB returned to Site 3 every summer from 2005, each year excavating a series of trenches placed parallel to the base of the cliffs to provide a cumulative cross-section of the deposits which lie beneath the sands. All of the excavations were hand-dug, and the excavated material was washed and sieved to ensure that all relevant artefacts and fossils were collected. Environmental samples were also taken to allow for the study of ancient pollen and analysis of the buried sediments. A

A public tour of the AHOB excavations on Happisburgh beach in June 2010, organised by the Coastal Heritage Project and the excavation team. Over 75 people come to view the excavations during the day, enjoying the chance to see the archaeologists at work and handle artefacts from the site. Barely a month later the results from the site made international headlines!

large number of flint tools were discovered during the excavations, most of them worked tools and flint cores from which flakes had been struck, and although some waste flakes were found there were so few of them as to suggest that the knapping of these tools occurred elsewhere. During the June 2010 excavation season, arrangements were made for the site to be opened up for public tours, so that the village's residents could view the trenches, hear about the project's results and handle some of the artefacts which had been discovered. The timing of these visits was particularly fortuitous, as shortly afterward the results of the first four years of the excavations were published in the journal *Nature* and quickly made headlines around the world (Parfitt *et al.* 2010).

The published results were truly staggering, indicating that human ancestors were occupying the Happisburgh area between 780,000 and 950,000 years ago – at least 80,000 years earlier than was previously thought, based on discoveries made at Site 1, and possibly as much as 250,000 years earlier. Therefore, the artefacts excavated from beneath Happisburgh beach are the earliest evidence for human occupation so far discovered in northern Europe! The preservation of bones, teeth, shells, beetle and plant remains at the site was also remarkably good, contributing greatly to our understanding of the site, and meaning that for the first time it was possible to reconstruct in great detail the environment in which these human ancestors were living, even down to the level of individual species of plants, trees and animals.

But how have these very early dates been

A late summer morning in Happisburgh during the Palaeolithic. A group of early humans are shown butchering a red deer on the floodplain of a large river. Approaching from the reed beds are two hyenas, eager to feed on the carcass. The commotion has startled a mare and her foals, who set-off to join their herd. Also attracted to the rich grassland vegetation are other herbivores, such as elk, red deer, bison and ancestral mammoths; voles, lemmings and mice scurry through the undergrowth and a beaver-like rodent, carrying sedges, heads to the safety of a small pool. The river provides a grassland corridor through an otherwise forested landscape. Woodland is dominated by pine and spruce, with a scattering of deciduous trees. (© John Sibbick/Ancient Human Occupation of Britain Project)

calculated? The flint artefacts recovered during these excavations cannot in themselves be dated, but they comprise simple flint flakes and are in no way as sophisticated as the handaxes which have been found loose on the beach or buried at Sites 1 and 2, suggesting that they predate them. Fortunately, several different methods can be used to date the geological layers in which they were discovered.

The Earth's magnetic field has not always pointed north as it does today, and on several occasions in the ancient past its polarity has reversed, so that the magnetic field pointed to what is now the south pole. Buried sediments preserve a record of the direction of the Earth's magnetism and we know from other research that the last time that this happened was the period from 950,000 years ago until 780,000 year ago. Scientific analyses of the deposits from which artefacts were recovered at Happisburgh indicated that the magnetic field of these layers was indeed reversed, meaning that the artefacts contained within them must be at least 780,000 years old and were possibly much older (Parfitt *et al.* 2010, 231).

The presence of certain species of animal and plant can be used for dating the period of occupation too. This is because the extinction dates of many of the species discovered – such as the southern mammoth – are known from the results of other research, as are the dates at which other species evolved, and so by correlating these different species it is possible to identify the period during which all of these old and new species could conceivably have been living side by side. The results of such analyses support the time-span indicated by the geo-magnetic evidence, also suggesting occupation between 950,000 and 780,000 years ago (Parfitt *et al.* 2010, 231).

Overall, the ecological evidence indicates that the climate was in the process of cooling during the time at which Happisburgh was occupied, making it broadly equivalent to the climate of modern-day Scandinavia. This, too, can provide an indication of date, as two known warm periods occurred during the broader time period indicated by the geo-magnetic and species-based evidence. These periods spanned 970–936,000 years ago and 866–814,000 years

ago, and conceivably Happisburgh could have been occupied during the later stages, that is, the colder end, of either of them. That human ancestors were living so far north in such cold conditions is significant in itself, as this had not previously been thought to be the case and raises important questions about the methods which these early humans used to adapt and survive in such inhospitable conditions (Parfitt *et al.* 2010, 231–2).

The excavated evidence also indicates that a large, slow river flowed through the Happisburgh area during this period, flanked by marshes and pools, stands of alder carr and surrounded by reed-swamp. A mixture of freshwater and saltwater species suggest that the estuary and salt marshes were not far away. Analysis of the gravels from this river channel revealed another startling conclusion – these gravels were found to be derived from south-eastern England, indicating that this river was in fact an ancestral version of the River Thames, flowing some 100km north of its current position at a time when a land-bridge still linked the south-east to mainland Europe (Parfitt *et al.* 2010, 229–31).

The publication of these results was met with great excitement in Happisburgh, especially among those residents who had visited the site and handled the artefacts earlier in the summer, and within hours of the news being announced the village sign had been suitably amended to say 'Happisburgh-on-Thames'. It is somewhat ironic that such internationally significant archaeological evidence should only be revealed by the erosion of the cliffs, but AHOB and others continue their research in the area with the promise of even more exciting results as further analyses are carried out on the excavated material.

Perhaps the most tantalising prospect is offered by the fact that, although flint tools have only provided indirect evidence for human occupation thus far, given the preservation of other fossils there is absolutely no reason why human remains could not lie waiting to be discovered beneath the shifting sands.

Chapter 3

Prehistoric and Roman Happisburgh

Following the period of very ancient human occupation discussed in the previous chapter, the Happisburgh area experienced the full ravages of the ice age. The retreating ice sheets deposited the loose glacial material which makes up the cliffs in the area, firmly burying the early human occupation evidence and effectively wiping the slate clean (Wymer 2005b). From the archaeological artefacts discovered in the parish, it would seem that humans only began to recolonise the area during the Mesolithic period – about 10,000 years ago – and it was not until the beginning of the Neolithic period, about 4,000 BC, that the Happisburgh area again began to see significant evidence for human activity.

Archaeological Evidence

There are several types of archaeological evidence which we can draw upon when attempting to reconstruct Happisburgh's prehistoric and Roman past. The first of these is archaeological excavation, where buried sites are carefully dug into and recorded, with any identifiable artefacts discovered during the process being used to ascribe dates to different features and layers. However, apart from the recent Ancient Human Occupation of Britain digs on the beach discussed in the previous chapter, Happisburgh has witnessed very few archaeological excavations. Of greater significance are the archaeological artefacts which have been collected from the ploughsoil during the extensive metal-detecting surveys which have been carried out in various parts of the parish over the last few decades. We are very fortunate in that the archaeological authorities

in Norfolk have always taken a very positive view of metal-detecting and since the 1970s they have worked closely with detectorists to encourage the proper recording of their finds. As a consequence, the Historic Environment Record contains details of literally tens of thousands of artefacts discovered across the county, and a sizable quantity have been discovered in Happisburgh. In addition to metal objects, detectorists working in Happisburgh have often collected flint, pottery and other artefacts from cultivated fields, where the action of the plough cutting into the ground and turning the soil brings buried objects onto the surface. Such objects allow a much greater understanding of the date and extent of the features which lie buried beneath and again the Historic Environment Record contains details of a number of such finds scatters from Happisburgh.

As well as objects plucked from the ground, a considerable amount of information about the past can be discovered from the air. When crops are planted over buried archaeological features, the nature of those features will affect the rate of growth of crops. For example, the rubble of a buried wall will create drier ground conditions, causing the crops planted above to be stunted and ripen more quickly than normal, whereas the remains of a silted-up ditch or pit will retain more moisture than the surrounding ground, meaning that crops planted above them will grow taller and ripen later than the rest of the crop. It should be stressed that cropmarks do not appear consistently and a number of factors can affect their appearance, including the type of crop sown and, especially, the amount of rainfall. Drier conditions increase the relative differences in moisture level which cause the crop-marks to appear, so drought summers are particularly good for cropmark formation (Wilson 2000, 67–86).

The cropmark phenomenon means that, at the appropriate point in the crop cycle, it is effectively possible for us to see a ground-plan of the buried archaeology picked out in the differential growth of the crop. Given that the kinds of archaeological features which cause cropmarks tend to be very large, they are best viewed from the air, where the bird's-eye view allows for much greater understanding of their form and layout. Archaeologists have been taking and making use of aerial photographs for many years, and the Norfolk Historic Environment Service maintains a library of aerial photographs of the county containing over 85,000 images dating from the early 20th century onwards.

Between 2001 and 2006, the team of aerial photograph interpreters employed by the Historic Environment Service undertook a systematic survey of aerial photographs of the entire Norfolk coast and used them to map, interpret and record all of the visible archaeological features (Albone *et al.* 2007). This work was undertaken as a part of English Heritage's National Mapping Programme and identified features dating from the Neolithic period to the Second World War. The results of this survey were fully integrated into the Norfolk Historic Environment Record, including digital maps and written descriptions of all of the observed features, and as a consequence we now have a detailed understanding of the buried archaeological remains in Happisburgh.

Prehistoric Flints

Numerous pieces of prehistoric worked flint have been found throughout the parish, both on the surface of ploughed fields and on the beaches, where they have fallen after being eroded from the cliffs. Unfortunately, very few of these flint artefacts have been sufficiently diagnostic for them to be ascribed to any particular period and most are recorded simply as being 'Prehistoric', i.e. belonging to the period

between the earliest human occupation and AD 42, after which date flint largely ceased to be used for tools. This uncertainty is understandable when one considers that the vast majority of the recorded material comprises flint flakes, that is, waste products produced during the making of flint tools, and as such they can tell us very little beyond the fact that prehistoric flint-working was occurring in the vicinity. Fortunately, mixed in amongst this material are a number of more datable and diagnostic artefacts which allow us to say more about the periods during which the parish was occupied and speculate on the nature of that occupation.

Mesolithic

The Mesolithic ('Middle Stone Age') spanned about 10,000 BC to 4,000 BC and is broadly defined as the period between the final retreat of the last of the glacial ice and the rise of agriculture-based societies, during which transient groups of hunter–gatherers roamed the region (Wymer 2005b). Despite the large quantities of prehistoric flint which have been discovered in the parish, only one example of a potentially Mesolithic flint blade has been identified, and even this identification is uncertain, as the blade could also be early Neolithic (NHER 35127).

Neolithic

The Neolithic ('New Stone Age') spanned approximately 4,000 BC until 2,400 BC. It was the period during which agriculture began to be practised and became the focus of more settled communities, who also began to engage in the manufacture of pottery and the creation of new types of earthwork monuments and funerary structures (Ashwin 2005a; 2005b). Although no Neolithic earthwork monuments or archaeological sites have been discovered in Happisburgh, the discoveries of a significant quantity of Neolithic flint artefacts are recorded in the Historic Environment Record, indicating that the Happisburgh area saw human activity during the Neolithic period.

Several late 19th- and early 20th-century documents record the discoveries in Happisburgh of Neolithic flint tools, although the locations at which these discoveries were made were not recorded beyond the name of the parish and cannot, therefore, be mapped (NHER 7082, 7083, 7084 and 28063). In more recent times, several identifiably Neolithic artefacts have been discovered in the parish, including near Whimpwell Green (NHER 17351), to the south of the lighthouse (NHER 32028) and north of the church (NHER 50074). Neolithic tools have also been found on the landward side of the parish, near Hall Farm (NHER 50116), to the west of Grub Street (NHER 50116) and from the vicinity of Walcott Green (NHER 51272). Tellingly, all of these artefacts have been discovered in locations which have also revealed a number of more undiagnostic flint flakes, suggesting that they too may be Neolithic in origin.

Of potentially much greater significance are a number of Neolithic flint axeheads which have been discovered on the seaward side of the parish, indicating that a substantial focus of Neolithic activity may yet still be discovered. Less optimistically, several other Neolithic axes have been discovered on the beach or in the remnants of cliff falls, presumably having been eroded from their original contexts on the clifftop, and it may be that any Neolithic sites have already been lost to the sea. The area around the lighthouse seems to have been a particular focus of activity: the broken butt of a partially polished flint axe exhibiting signs having been severely fire damaged was discovered east of the lighthouse in 1996 (NHER 31461); a more complete polished axe with damage to its cutting edge was found south of the lighthouse in 1997 (NHER 34924); and an exceptionally large polished axe in near-pristine condition was discovered on the beach east of the lighthouse in 2010 (NHER 53995).

Other finds from this area of the beach include the broken blade of a polished axe and a more complete, but sea-rolled axe, both of which were found at the foot of the cliffs in front of Beach Road during the severe erosion of the late 1990s (NHER 36826). Further to the south, a particularly fine and quite large example of a Late Neolithic polished axe was discovered on

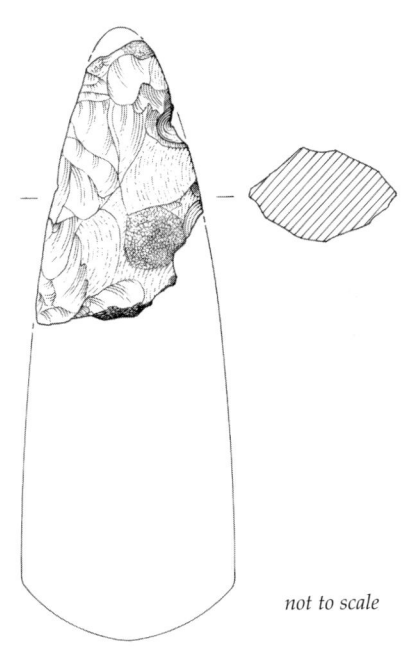

not to scale

Fire-cracked Neolithic polished flint axe discovered near the lighthouse in 1996, original height approx 16cm. (NHER 31461; drawn by Jason Gibbons, after Peter Robins)

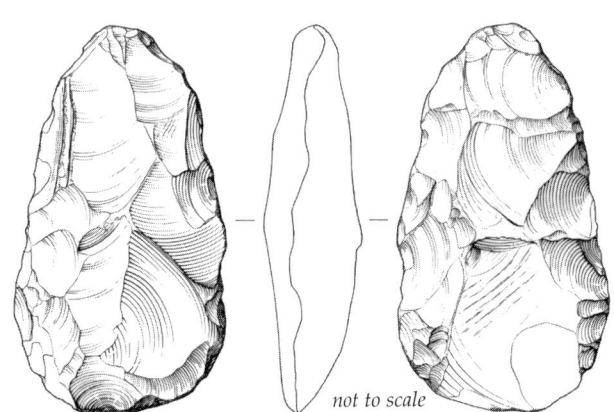

not to scale

A flaked Neolithic flint axe discovered below the end of Beach Road in early 2011 by members of the Happisburgh Heritage Group, height approx 10cm. (NHER 55391; drawn by Jason Gibbons)

the beach 'between Happisburgh village and Cart Gap' in 2004 (NHER 40892). Another flint axe, this time flaked rather than polished and possibly unfinished, was discovered below the end of Beach Road in early 2011 by members of the Happisburgh Heritage Group (NHER 55391).

That so many of these discoveries have been made in the vicinity of the lighthouse and the cliffs to its east suggests that the high ground on which the lighthouse stands may well have been a significant focus of activity during the Neolithic period. While it is possible that this activity was of a domestic nature, the type of artefacts recovered seem to suggest it was more likely that this activity was of a funerary character, perhaps focussing around an earth-work long barrow in which communal burials took place. The reasoning behind this is the fact that several of the polished axes which have been recovered are of an exceptionally high quality and show little or no sign of having been used for any functional purpose, suggesting that they were prestige items intended for ceremonial purposes and were perhaps used as grave-goods. It is frustrating, but we are likely never to get a satisfactory answer to this question, as in all likelihood the evidence has already been lost to the sea.

Bronze Age

The Bronze Age (approximately 2,400 BC to 700 BC) was the period during which flint tools began to be replaced with copper-alloy – bronze – tools, and during which changes in funerary practice saw the introduction of new kinds of

earthwork monuments. Agricultural practice and woodland clearance also seem to have increased during this period, as settlements became more firmly established (Ashwin 2005b; 2005c).

The Bronze Age is the first archaeological period for which traces of earthwork monuments survive in Happisburgh. Studying the aerial photographs of the parish, the National Mapping Programme recorded the cropmarks of ten ring-ditches measuring between 12m and 30m in diameter, and thought to be the ploughed-out remains of Bronze Age burial mounds (NHER 38729, 38731, 38735, 38736, 38767, 38768, 38771, 38774, 38775 and 38779). These burial mounds – barrows – would have each comprised a circular mound of earth perhaps as much as a couple of metres high which was heaped up over the burial of a Bronze Age individual. The earth to make the mound was usually dug out from a circular quarry-ditch surrounding the barrow, and it is this ditch which is later visible as a cropmark. Eight of the Happisburgh barrows appear to have a single ditch, one has two concentric ditches (NHER 38779), while another certainly

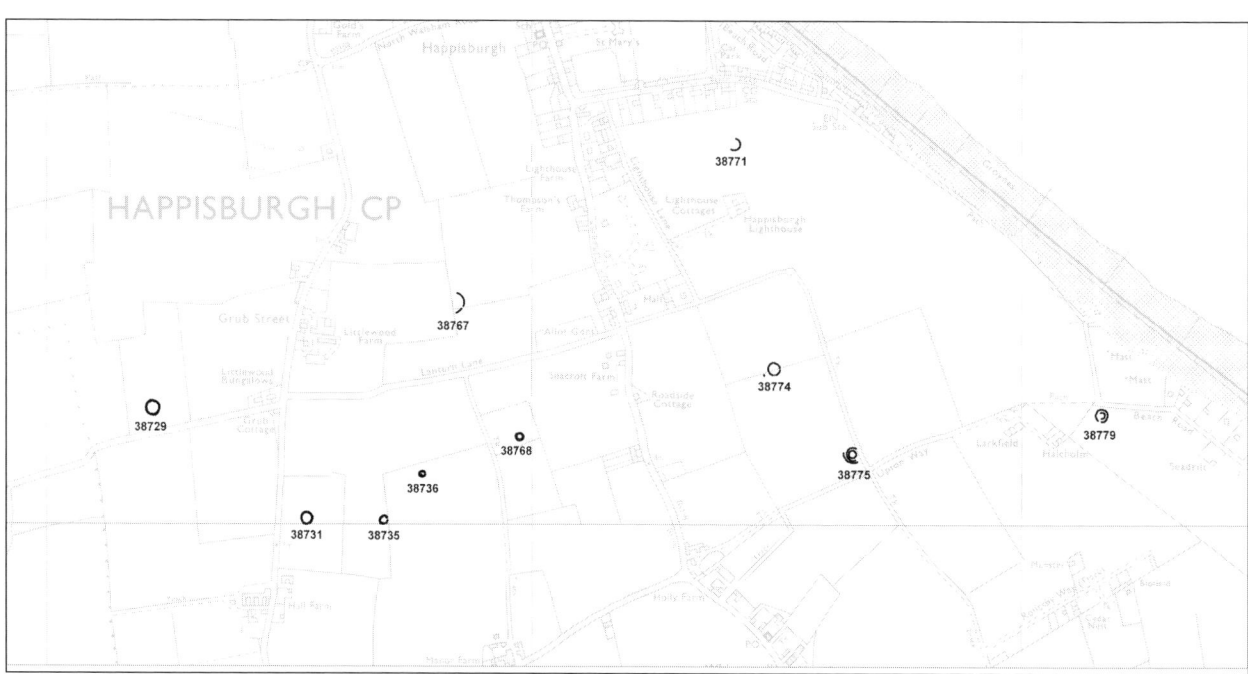

The distribution of probable Bronze Age round-barrows recorded by the National Mapping Programme. Note how the barrows are clustered in the lower ground to the south of the lighthouse. (Cropmark transcriptions © English Heritage/Norfolk County Council; Mapping © Crown copyright and database rights 2011 Ordnance Survey 100019340)

An aerial view looking north showing Bronze Age ring-ditch NHER 38774 with Happisburgh lighthouse in the background taken in June 1996. Note how the ring ditch is cut in half by the more recent field boundary. (© Norfolk County Council; Photograph by D.A. Edwards: TG3830/AT/JFD6)

has two concentric ditches and may have three (NHER 38775). There is archaeological evidence for many hundreds of Bronze Age round barrows in Norfolk, a large number of which survived as earthworks until the latter half of the 20th century before being ploughed flat in the process of agricultural development (Ashwin 2005b, 19–20).

A near-vertical aerial view looking north showing Bronze Age ring-ditch NHER 38775 taken in June 1996. Note how the cropmarks indicate the existence of two, and possibly three, concentric ring-ditches. (© Norfolk County Council; Photograph by D.A. Edwards: TG3830/ABA/JFD13)

The ten Happisburgh barrows lie in a broad cluster and collectively form a barrow cemetery (NHER 55788), an arrangement which is typical of patterns observed in Norfolk and elsewhere, and which indicates that the Happisburgh area was a choice spot for burial for a prolonged period during the Bronze Age. All of the barrows lie within the band of slightly lower-lying ground to the south of Beach Road and the north of Whimpwell Green, perhaps the base of a former river valley, and this landscape setting is also typical. Bronze Age barrows tend to be located on the higher reaches of the sides of river valleys, often overlooking the heads or confluences of the rivers, and they are often sited in such a way as to have been clearly visible silhouetted against the sky when viewed by those living lower down in the valley. The possible existence of Neolithic funerary monuments in the area, as might be indicated by the polished axes, may also be a factor in the location of the Bronze Age barrows, as Bronze Age barrow cemeteries are often focussed around an earlier Neolithic long barrow (Albone *et al.* 2007, 47–53).

As might be expected, given the existence of the barrow cemetery, several Bronze Age artefacts have also been discovered in the parish. Tellingly, many of these artefacts have been found in the vicinity of the ring-ditches and may well be derived from the ploughed-out barrows themselves, as it was often the case that grave-goods were buried with the deceased. Again, while some of these artefacts have been recovered from the ploughed fields, others have been found on the beach, suggesting that other Bronze Age monuments have already been eroded.

The point of a particularly fine Bronze Age sword or rapier was found on the clifftop in 1982 in a location east of the lighthouse which has subsequently been lost to the sea (NHER 18519). The surviving fragment comprises the end one-third of the sword's blade, and the drawing published here includes a reconstructed outline of the rest of the sword, which is of a recognised type and shape. It has been suggested that such swords would never have been used as functional items, as the blades could be very flimsy and the cutting edges often show little or no sign of having been used (Darvill 1987, 129). It is likely that they might have served more ceremonial purposes, demonstrating

wealth and authority, in a manner akin to the unusually large and highly polished Neolithic axeheads found elsewhere in the parish.

Woodworking and the clearing of woodland were clearly important activities during the Bronze Age, and large numbers of axes of various types, as well as chisels and other tools have been discovered across the county (Ashwin 2005c). An early Bronze Age flanged axehead with a flat blade was found on the beach to the east of the lighthouse in 1995 (NHER 34500). This axehead would have originally been hafted onto a wooden handle and had received considerable damage to its cutting edge, much of which was missing, suggesting that it had been used extensively. A second Bronze Age axe was found in the field to the south of Lighthouse Close in 1998 (NHER 34331). This axe is of the socketed variety, in that it has a hollow socket in its top into which a protuberance on the end of the wooden handle would be inserted to create a more solid haft. The location of this findspot lies broadly equidistant between two of the cropmark ring-ditches – NHER 38768 and 38774 – and may well be related to their use. The blade of a Bronze

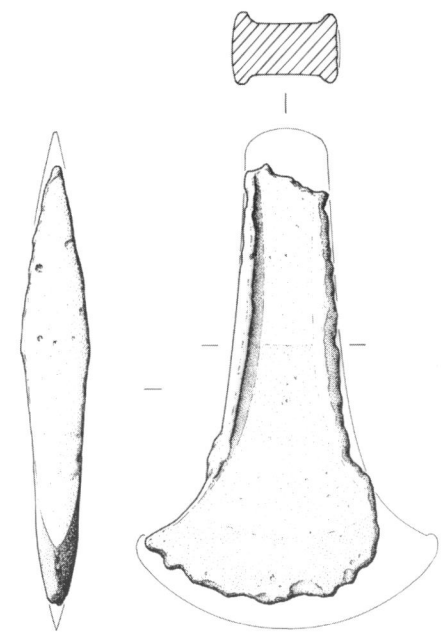

not to scale: original height approx 11cm

A Bronze Age sword or rapier found on the clifftop in 1982, showing the reconstructed profile of the missing portion of the blade and handle, estimated original length 60cm. (NHER 18519; drawn by Jason Gibbons)

not to scale

The Bronze Age flat-bladed axehead found on the beach to the east of the lighthouse in 1995. (NHER 34500; drawn by Jason Gibbons)

35

Age chisel was found immediately to the east of the lighthouse in 2005 (NHER 31461), near to a possible ploughed-out barrow (NHER 38771). Like the second of the Bronze Age axeheads, this chisel had a socket so that a wooden handle could be inserted into its top.

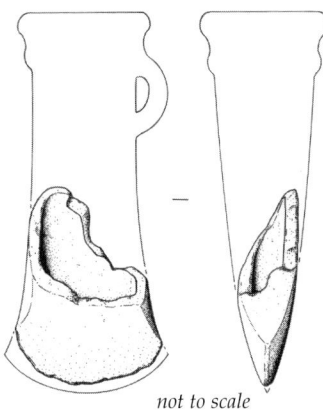

not to scale

The Bronze Age socketed axe found to the south of Lighthouse Close in 1998, estimated original length approx. 10cm. (NHER 34331; drawn by Jason Gibbons)

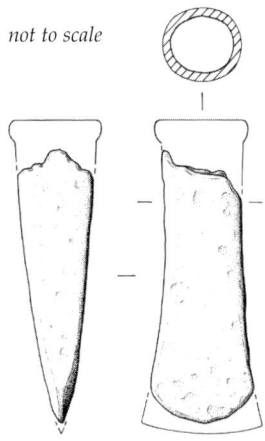

not to scale

The blade of a Bronze Age chisel discovered immediately to the east of the lighthouse in 2005, estimated original length approx. 8cm. (NHER 31461; drawn by Jason Gibbons)

Although copper-alloy replaced flint for many tools, flint still continued to be used for tools such as scrapers and arrowheads, some of which can be identified with certainty as being Bronze Age. A flint scraper was found in association with the copper-alloy chisel near Grub Street (NHER 23411), while further Bronze Age flintwork has been found in the fields to the east of St Mary's/Happisburgh Manor (NHER 33430) and near to Mill Farm (NHER 50273).

As with the Neolithic evidence, there is a definite concentration of Bronze Age monuments and artefacts in the central part of Happisburgh parish, focussing on the slightly lower ground to the south of the lighthouse. The identification of the cropmarks of a Bronze Age barrow cemetery is significant, and indicates that the Happisburgh area was an important focus of funerary practices during this period.

Iron Age and Roman Periods
The Iron Age (700 BC until AD 43) and the Roman period (AD 43 to 410) are considered here together, because the chronological division between the two periods, which is dictated by the date of the Roman invasion of Britain, is not reflected clearly in the archaeological record. As the name suggests, the Iron Age saw the introduction of iron, but it also saw the introduction of coinage, an even greater intensification of agriculture and significant changes in funerary practices and the organisation of settlements and fields (Hutcheson and Ashwin 2005; Hutcheson 2005). The Roman invasion brought about significant changes in the nature of the everyday material culture, including the introduction of masonry buildings, better quality pottery and the widespread use of coinage, as well as bringing towns, villas and news roads to the East Anglian landscape. However, in the more rural areas the settlement evidence suggests a much greater degree of continuity between the Iron Age and the Roman periods than might otherwise be supposed, with many local farmsteads continuing largely unchanged throughout both periods (Gurney 2005).

Very little Iron Age material has been discovered in Happisburgh, those artefacts which have been discovered primarily being sherds of pottery. The locations of these sherds suggest that Iron Age activity may have been limited to a few discrete areas of the parish: a few sherds have been discovered in the field to the south of the lighthouse (NHER 32028), others have been discovered to the south and west of Littlewood Bungalows (NHER 51394 and 51498), and several of the fields adjacent to Hall Farm have also produced sherds, suggesting that a much larger Iron Age site may lie in that vicinity (NHER 50077, 50116, 50117 and 51188). It is particularly telling that all of the locations at which sherds of Iron Age pottery have been discovered have also produced Roman pottery, coins and other metalwork, indicating that these sites continued to be occupied into the Roman period. Additional surface scatters of Roman material have been discovered in the vicinity of the lighthouse (NHER 31461 and 34330), north of Lantern Lane (NHER 55118), near to Holly Farm (NHER 35127), near Thatchers (NHER 34410), on the beach (NHER 40528), and at Cart Gap, where a Roman brooch and rather unusual cylindrical weight have been discovered (NHER 52817 and 53782).

The National Mapping Programme has identified the cropmark remains of two possible Iron Age and/or Romano-British farmsteads in Happisburgh, one immediately to the west of Littlewood Cottages in the western part of the parish (NHER 38730) and one immediately to the east of Whimpwell Green (NHER 38744). The Littlewood Cottages farmstead comprises an enclosure with an internal subdivision and lying adjacent to a north–south trackway, but aligned slightly differently to the main field-system (NHER 38730). It is possible that this enclosure is an earlier or later element within the cropmark complex, although it is probably of Iron Age to Roman date. The farmstead is associated with one of the Iron Age pottery scatters discussed above, and is also the location of a number of discoveries of Roman pottery and metalwork, including furniture fittings, brooches, vessels and a cosmetic pestle for grinding make-up pigment (NHER 51394, 51498 and 53801). Particularly significant is the discovery of a copper-alloy brooch fragment with traces of the clay mould in which it was cast still adhering to it, indicating that brooches, at least, were being manufactured on the site (NHER 51394).

The cropmarks of a second farmstead comprising two small rectangular enclosures have been identified immediately to the east of Whimpwell Green (NHER 38744), and Whimpwell Green is also the site of additional

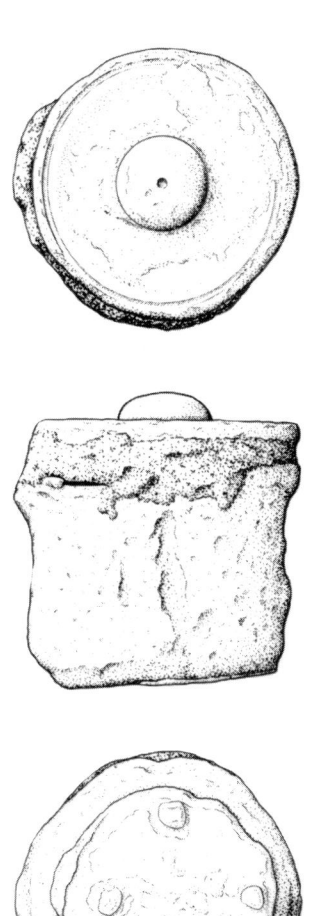

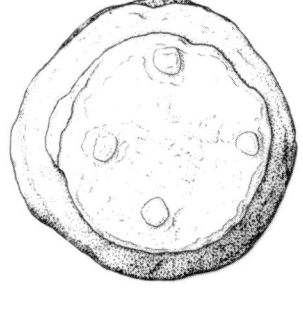

not to scale: original height approx 2.5cm

An unusual Roman copper-alloy weight discovered near Cart Gap in 2009. The weight is 54g, the equivalent of two unciae, *a Roman unit of measurement. (NHER 53782; drawn by Jason Gibbons)*

discoveries of Roman coins and pottery (NHER 17351 and 37717). Both of these farmsteads sit within an extensive network of other cropmarks revealed by the National Mapping Programme. These cropmarks have been identified as the archaeological remains of extensive Iron Age and Roman agricultural field-systems with tracks on the basis of their shape, size and relationship to other landscape features. However, without archaeological excavations to test these interpretations it is difficult to be sure of these identifications and due caution must be exercised (NHER 36495, 36765, 38585, 38585, 38726, 38739, 38739, 38742, 38744, 38745, 38746 and

An aerial photograph looking north taken in June 1996 showing the cropmarks of possible Iron Age/Romano-British farmstead (NHER 38730) in the foreground and the cropmark of a Bronze Age ring-ditch beyond (NHER 38729). (© Norfolk County Council; Photograph by D.A. Edwards: TG3730/L/JFE9)

The cropmarks of the possible Iron Age/Romano-British farmstead (NHER 38730), as identified by the National Mapping Programme. The cropmarks of the enclosure are picked out in black, while the cropmarks of the surrounding field-system are in grey. (Cropmark transcriptions © English Heritage/Norfolk County Council; Mapping © Crown copyright and database rights 2011 Ordnance Survey 100019340)

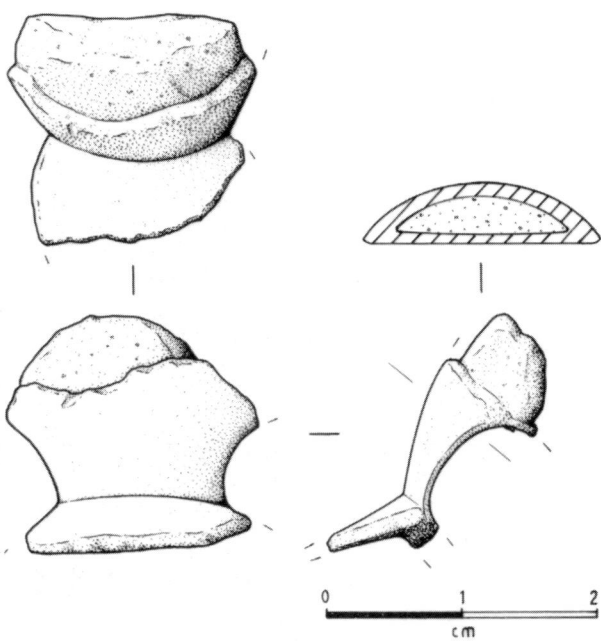

A fragment of a copper-alloy Roman brooch with traces of the clay mould in which it was cast still adhering to it. (NHER 51394; drawn by Jason Gibbons)

lished in the prehistoric period and then continuing to be used.

On the basis of the archaeological evidence discussed here it is clear that, at the very least, the Happisburgh area was home to at least two Iron Age/Romano-British farmsteads, both of which were potentially set within substantial tracts of planned field-systems, although it is difficult to be more certain about this association. Results of the kind discovered in Happisburgh are very typical of the evidence which has been identified during the National Mapping Programme's systematic study of aerial photographs, the results of which would seem to suggest that large parts of the county were being cultivated during the later Iron Age and Romano-British periods to a much greater intensity than had previously been supposed. In some instances, these early field-systems provided the framework on which later field-systems developed, whereas in other places the later fields bear little resemblance to these earlier phases. The fact that in Happisburgh so many traces of fields are visible from the air and not obscured by later boundaries would seem to suggest the latter is the case here.

38769). It is likely that most of these field systems developed over several hundreds of years, with dominant alignments being estab-

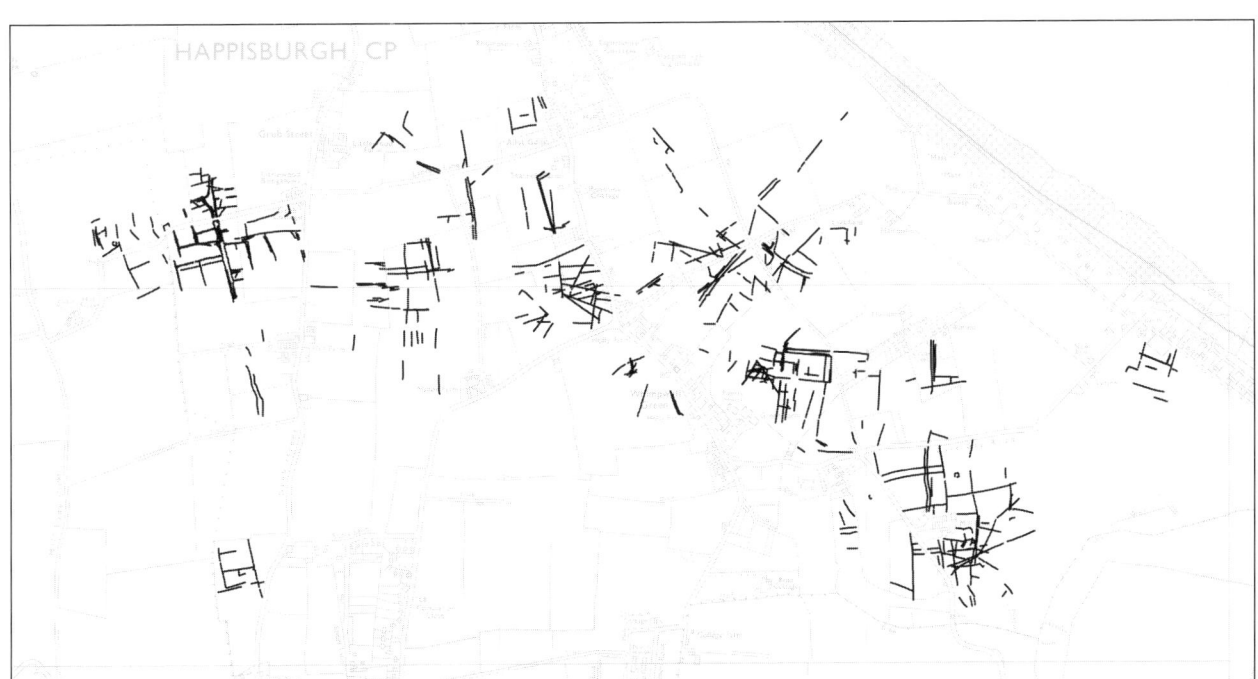

The possible traces of Iron Age/Romano-British fields in Happisburgh, as recorded by the National Mapping Programme. (Cropmark transcriptions © English Heritage/Norfolk County Council; Mapping © Crown copyright and database rights 2011 Ordnance Survey 100019340)

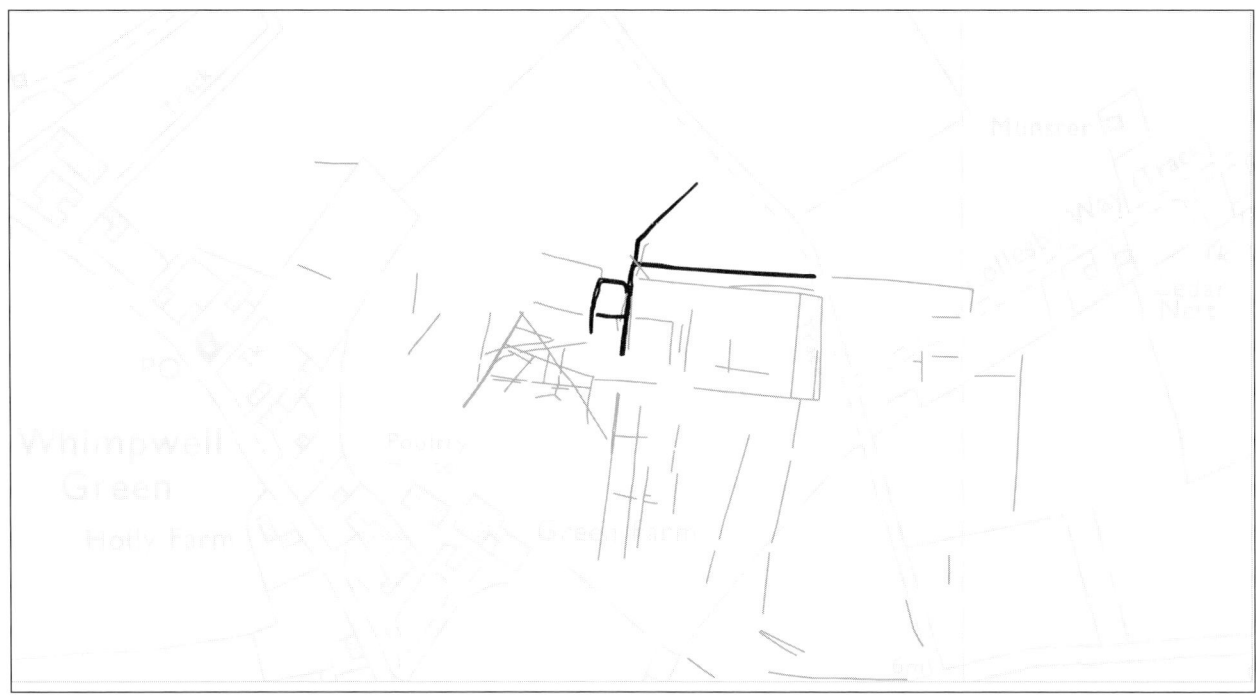

The cropmarks of the possible Iron Age/Romano-British farmstead (NHER 38744), as identified by the National Mapping Programme. The cropmarks of the enclosure are picked out in black, while the cropmarks of the surrounding field-system are in grey. (Cropmark transcriptions © English Heritage/Norfolk County Council; Mapping © Crown copyright and database rights 2011 Ordnance Survey 100019340)

An aerial photograph looking south taken in July 1977 showing the cropmarks of possible Iron Age/Romano-British farmstead (NHER 38744). (© Norfolk County Council; Photograph by D.A. Edwards: TG3829/A/AKJ5)

Chapter 4

Anglo-Saxon and Medieval Happisburgh

It is generally accepted that the Roman period ended in the early decades of the fifth century, when the Roman authorities withdrew their administration and, more significantly, their army from Britain in order to concentrate on the defence of Rome from barbarian invaders (Wacher 1998, 295–300). Into this vacuum came settlers from the coastal lands of north-western Europe and Scandinavia, who brought with them a very different material culture, and within a couple of centuries East Anglia was thoroughly Anglo-Saxon in character. There has been much debate about the nature of this migration, particularly regarding how many people may have actually migrated and whether their settlement was peaceful or violent. However, as with the transition from the Iron Age to the Roman period, the vast majority of the population appear to have continued to live the same lives as they always had, albeit with a new material culture (Williamson 1993, 49–72; Penn 2005).

From an archaeological point of view, the break from Rome is very clear to see, as the production of coinage ceased, societies lapsed back to using handmade pottery and timber again became the preferred building material, effectively rendering many Anglo-Saxon buildings archaeologically invisible. Funerary practices changed dramatically too, with cremation and furnished burial both being practised during the Early Anglo-Saxon period, before the arrival of Christianity in the seventh century (Hoggett 2010, 1–6, 81–115).

A great restructuring of the landscape occurred during the Middle Anglo-Saxon period – broadly the mid-seventh to mid-ninth centuries – which saw the establishment of the features and institutions which were to shape the English landscape for much of the next thousand years. Foremost among these changes was the major dislocation of settlements, which saw numerous and disparate Early Anglo-Saxon settlements coalesce into more permanent nucleated settlements, most of them the precursors of the villages which we know today, Happisburgh being no exception (Rippon 2008, 138–200). Closely bound up with these changes was the establishment of the church, which has remained firmly at the heart of village life in Happisburgh ever since (Hoggett 2010, 116–62).

Early Anglo-Saxon

The Early Anglo-Saxon period broadly spans the fifth to the seventh centuries AD, during which time the Roman influence faded and Anglo-Saxon culture took hold. As was referred to above, it is difficult to see the Early Anglo-Saxons in the archaeological record very clearly, but enough artefacts have been discovered in Happisburgh to indicate an Early Anglo-Saxon presence in the parish. As might be expected, several artefacts have been discovered in the vicinity of the Roman farmsteads discussed in the previous chapter, suggesting that a degree of occupation continued at those sites which would be very much in keeping with patterns observed elsewhere in the county. A copper-alloy brooch was recovered from the site of the Whimpwell Green farmstead (NHER 17351), while a broken fragment of another brooch was found not far away to the south (NHER 49809), as was a quantity of possibly Early Anglo-Saxon pottery (NHER 50273). Early Anglo-Saxon material has also been discovered at the Littlewood Bungalows farmstead site, including fragments of a copper-alloy brooch (NHER 51394) and just over the parish boundary into East Ruston, where an intricately carved die or stamp which would have been used during the Early Anglo-Saxon period to impress a design into gold sheet in order to produce pendants (NHER 52736). This is an incredibly rare type of object, and is one which indicates that high-status metalworking was taking place in or near Happisburgh at this time.

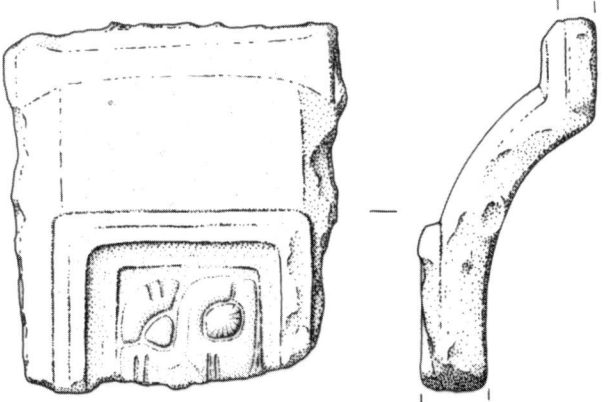

A broken fragment of an Early Saxon cruciform brooch, shown larger than actual size. (NHER 49809; Drawn by Jason Gibbons)

In addition to stray finds, there is a possibility that Early Anglo-Saxon buildings might also survive in the parish. The air photo interpreters working for English Heritage's National Mapping Programme suggested that a group of three small rectangular pits measuring 2–2.5m wide by 4–6m long located in the fields near to the lighthouse might be the remains of Early Anglo-Saxon buildings (NHER 16015). Known as Grubenhäuser – 'grub huts' – or sunken-featured buildings, when excavated this type of structure comprises a hollow dug into

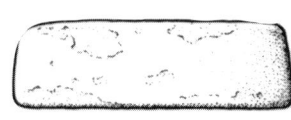

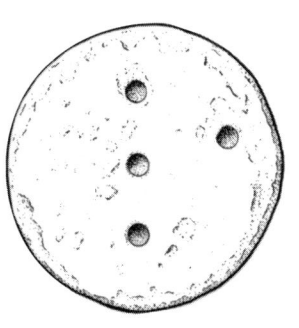

not to scale: diameter approx 2cm

An unusual Early Saxon die or stamp for the manufacture of gold-foil pendants. (NHER 52736; Drawn by Jason Gibbons)

the earth surrounded by post-holes, where wooden posts have rotted *in situ* leaving a dark stain. When these structures first began to be excavated in the 1930s it was thought that the Anglo-Saxons must have constructed rudimentary roofs over these hollows and lived in them, hence their being dubbed 'grub huts', but more recent excavations at sites such as West Stow in Suffolk have indicated that these hollows were effectively the cellars beneath a suspended timber floor, above which was constructed a much more conventional timber building (Tipper 2004). Being timber, of course, only those parts of the building which were cut into the ground – the cellar and the supporting posts – survive in the archaeological record. If indeed there is an Early Anglo-Saxon settlement on the clifftops at Happisburgh, then it is possible that some of the ditches discussed in the previous chapter as being potentially Iron Age and/or Romano-British may also be also be Early Anglo-Saxon (NHER 16015).

These possible buildings lie close to the clifftop, and there are indications from elsewhere in the parish that further Early Anglo-Saxon evidence has already been destroyed by erosion. A gilded sleeve-clasp, a kind of Early Anglo-Saxon cufflink, has been found close to the edge of the cliff in the fields to the north of the church (NHER 24004) and a rather spectacular pyramid-shaped silver mount inset with a garnet and through which a leather strap would have been threaded was found to the north of Cart Gap, having apparently fallen onto the beach from the cliff (NHER 51527).

We know from studies of the landscape settings of Early Anglo-Saxon settlements and cemeteries that the two elements were deliberately kept separate, although they could lie in close proximity to one another. We also know that Early Anglo-

Reconstructed sunken-featured buildings at West Stow in Suffolk. The building on the left shows the original interpretation of the 'grub hut', while the building on the right shows a more conventional style of building. Archaeologically, the footprint of the two buildings is the same.

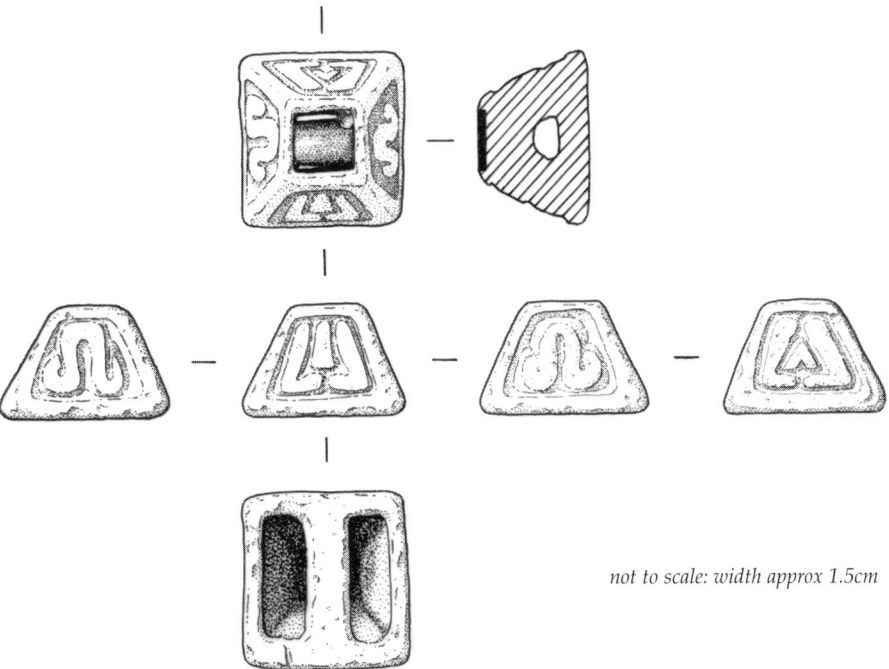

not to scale: width approx 1.5cm

A garnet-inset silver mount, through which a leather strap would have been threaded, shown larger than actual size. (NHER 51527; Drawn by Jason Gibbons)

Saxon burials were often deliberately located near to Bronze Age barrows, sometimes even being dug into the surviving earthwork mound (Hoggett 2010, 117–30). If, as seems likely, occupation continued at the two Romano-British farmsteads into the Early Anglo-Saxon period, and that a third settlement may have been established on the clifftops near to the lighthouse, then there is a strong likelihood that the earthwork mounds of the Bronze Age barrow cemetery may well have become the focus of Early Anglo-Saxon burials too. Although no direct evidence for this has been discovered so far, the exceptional quality of some of the stray finds discovered to date strongly hints at this being the case.

Middle and Late Anglo-Saxon

The Middle (AD 650–850) and Late Anglo-Saxon (AD 850–1066) periods mark a significant threshold in the archaeological record for many of the region's villages, as these are the periods during which many of the settlements which went on to become medieval and modern villages were founded. We are particularly fortunate in that these periods saw the re-introduction of well-made pottery which was widely used, so that we can take its presence to be a reliable indicator of occupation. The first of these pottery types is Ipswich Ware, which was produced in Ipswich from the mid-seventh until the mid-ninth centuries, before it was superseded by Thetford-type Wares, produced in Thetford and other places from the mid-ninth century onwards. These two periods also saw the use of many very closely datable items of metalwork, which we can also use to date the foundation and development of the early settlement. Of course, given that the later village continued to develop on the same spot, it is sometimes difficult for us to be able to study the remains of the features which lie buried beneath the later houses, but occasionally objects are found in flowerbeds and during building works which provide us with a glimpse of what lies beneath.

Unlike those archaeological periods discussed thus far, the material record from the Middle Anglo-Saxon period onwards comprises a great deal of material – far too much to easily be discussed here on an object-by-object or site-by-site basis – although anyone interested in the details of this material can find out more by visiting the *Norfolk Heritage Explorer* website. Suffice it to say that the fields surrounding the core of the village contain plenty of material evidence to support the suggestion that Happisburgh was occupied from the seventh century onwards: sherds of Ipswich Ware and several pieces of Middle Anglo-Saxon metalwork have been found in the parish, as have considerably larger quantities of Thetford-type ware sherds and Late Anglo-Saxon metalwork. Having relied thus far on the material record to tell the story of Happisburgh, the Middle and Late Anglo-Saxon periods are the first time during which we are able to draw upon more conventional historical sources, including the study of place-names and the contents of the Domesday Book.

The Origins of Happisburgh

by Tim Pestell (Norfolk Museums and Archaeology Service)

Although there had been occupation in Happisburgh from the very earliest times, as we have seen, the period from which this spot on the Norfolk coast first became known by the name we still call it today – Happisburgh – belongs to the post-seventh century Anglo-Saxon period. The name is first seen in the Domesday Book of 1086 (of which more below) where it is written as *Hapesburc*, meaning 'Hæp's burg'. This in itself needs some explanation. The personal name Hæp is relatively uncontroversial, being an Anglo-Saxon name, seen also in the place-name Hapsford in Cheshire, there meaning 'Hæp's ford'. The *-burg* element is more complex, as it suggests a defensive enclosure of some kind, the word deriving from the Old English word *burh*, a fortified place (Sandred *et al.* 1996, 92–3). However, in some cases it is clear this could mean no more than a fortified manor, rather than a full-scale fort. If we are to look for where such a site may have been we need to look over the entire parish. First, though, we should consider some wider landscape evidence.

In the Anglo-Saxon period, the countryside was organised in various ways. Perhaps the most important change after the collapse of Roman authority in Britain was the breakdown of the old Roman estates and by the seventh century, the formation of new ones. These provided a means for the new Anglo-Saxon aristocrats and rulers to run the countryside, and saw huge areas of land forming estates that could cover what are today a number of different parishes (Reynolds 1999, 65–110). It is therefore interesting to note that the local Hundred – another, larger unit of land used for administration – is called the Happing Hundred. Once again, this points to modern Happisburgh having been of some former local importance early on. Happing means 'the followers of Hæp' or 'Hæp's people' and this type of place-name referring to people is one of only three found in Norfolk (the others are Loddon, meaning 'the people of the Lodne' and Clavering Hundred,

'the people of Cnava'). It may be, then, that Happisburgh once formed some sort of tribal area in the earliest Anglo-Saxon period, which subsequently developed as the administrative centre of a wider area.

If there had been some sort of enclosure forming the centre of a large early estate, where might this have been? A possibility – and with our present understanding of the village's archaeology it is no more than that – is that it was based on the knoll on which the church now stands. Not only would such a centre be an obvious place to build a church, but the actual churchyard is a large one. This is potentially important as the earliest Anglo-Saxon churches, called minsters, also served far wider areas than modern parishes (Blair 2005, 79–134). As a result, they usually needed large churchyards to provide the space to bury all the dead from such a wide area. Although not proof, Happisburgh's large churchyard may be an indication of its

Happisburgh church from the air in 1984, showing the high ground on which the church sits and the very large churchyard. (© Norfolk County Council; Photograph by D.A. Edwards: TG3731/D/AXR18)

former importance as a minster serving a large estate in the Happing Hundred.

Finally, the land boundaries and roads in the region of the church are quite rectilinear, and might possibly suggest a former rectangular earthwork, perhaps a *burh*, which had stood here and helped to influence the layout and direction of the surrounding roads. Whimpwell Street, the main road into the village from the south, is notably straight, but then veers at a right-angle to the west, with another road running to the east up to the Hill House pub. With the rectangular extent of the churchyard and another road, Blacksmith's Lane, which also existed at least as early as 1834 when it was shown on the tithe map of Happisburgh, running to the north, these help to create a rectilinear block of land. Might this be the ghost outline of a former enclosure around the hilltop here – perhaps even Hæp's burh?

Members of the Happisburgh Heritage Group examine the 1834 tithe map of the parish during a recent visit to the Norfolk Record Office.

Domesday Happisburgh

The Domesday Book was the product of a survey instigated in 1085 by William the Conqueror in order to establish the extent of his newly acquired lands and record the ownership and occupancy of the whole of England. In order to complete the survey, the country was divided into a series of circuits, each visited by a different team of commissioners. These commissioners heard testimony from royal officials, gathered information from local juries and received written accounts from tenants-in-chief

and their findings were collated into the Domesday Book. It is less well known that Domesday Book is actually two books, referred to as Great and Little Domesday Books respectively. The majority of the country is recorded in Great Domesday Book, which is largely the work of one scribe and was edited into a consistent format. Little Domesday Book, on the other hand, is the product of a number of scribes and its entries survive in a largely unedited form and consequently provide a lot of detail about the manors it describes. We are incredibly fortunate that it is the Little Domesday Book which covers Norfolk, Suffolk and Essex, meaning that we are able to understand a great deal more about the eastern region's 11th-century settlements (Roffe 2000).

It should be stressed that the Domesday Book recorded manors, and not settlements, so there are actually two entries in the Little Domesday Book relating to Happisburgh (Alecto 2002). The first, and larger entry, is listed under the landholdings of the King, William the Conqueror, and records that Happisburgh's main manor was held by Edric in the time of Edward the Confessor, King before the Norman conquest of 1066. Edric had extensive landholdings throughout East Anglia at the time of the Domesday survey and the area of his Happisburgh manor is given as 13 carucates, the carucate being a Domesday measurement of land thought to be broadly equivalent to the area which could be ploughed with an eight-ox team.

The population of the manor is given as 21 villagers and 20 smallholders, with three slaves, although as only men were recorded in these reckonings the actual population of the manor at this time may be four or five times these figures. The survey records that three plough-teams were kept on the lord's own land within the manor, and that at the time of the Conquest there were nine other plough-teams belonging to the general populace, although this number had reduced to seven plough, by the time of the Domesday survey in 1086. Regarding the landscape and livestock of the estate, the survey listed ten acres of meadow and enough woodland for 16 pigs (although, again, we remain

This photograph of the back of page 133 of the Little Domesday Book shows the entry for Happisburgh under the landholdings of King William. The Happisburgh entry begins on line four. (© Alecto Historical Editions)

The second entry for Happisburgh on page 150 of the Little Domesday Book, under the holdings of Count Alan. The entry begins on line two. (© Alecto Historical Editions) unsure how much woodland a pig actually needed). Four head of cattle, 18 pigs and 200 sheep are also recorded.

Also within the manor there were 21 freemen who held 86 acres of land, possibly in a hamlet or outlying settlement. At the Conquest, these freemen had five plough-teams, but this then reduced to four. Another 12 freemen, who had allegiance to Edric, held four carucates of land with eight villagers, nine smallholders and one slave. Overall, they had ten plough-teams at the Conquest, although this had fallen to nine by 1086. Half a carucate of this holding had apparently been annexed from these freemen by another Edric, one of Count Alan's men (of which more below). These freemen had apparently been added to the manor by Earl Ralph of East Anglia, an English lord who had held this Happisburgh manor for a time after the Conquest, but who forfeited his lands when he rebelled against the King in 1075.

The whole of this first manor was valued as having been worth £7 in 1066, with the freemen's holdings being valued separately at 40s. When Earl Ralph held the manor it was worth £10, and at the time of the Domesday survey in 1086 it was valued at £16-20s and apparently measured 1½ leagues in length and the same in width, and the holder of the manor had to pay 30d in exactions.

A final note in this entry states that Robert Malet, High Sheriff of Norfolk and Suffolk, had a claim of the manor, stating that his father William, a companion of William I, had held it before he 'went into the marsh' to hunt for Hereward the Wake, during which hunt he was killed. The Hundred court apparently testified to this fact, but the Domesday record also states that William Malet was not holding this land on the day on which he died.

A second, much shorter, Domesday entry appears under the landholdings of Count Alan, Duke of Brittany. It states that at the time of the Conquest there were two freemen holding 100 acres of land in Happisburgh, of which 60 acres had been in the possession of the main Happisburgh manor at the time of Earl Ralph's forfeiture of his lands in 1075. The entry indicates that Edric had seized the lands at this point and that he vouched for its occupants, one Ivo Taillebois and his associates. This might suggest that Edric was attempting to retake some of his lands after the main Happisburgh manor had been taken from him, and it is possible that such actions here and elsewhere may have ultimately led to his being exiled. The original 100 acre holding had presumably been reunited under Count Alan, and had five smallholders and one plough. Its valuation was split between the first 60 acres, worth 6s, and the remaining 40 acres, valued at 4s.

Wymondham Abbey

During the medieval period Happisburgh was one of the largest estates owned by Wymondham priory, an important connection which linked Happisburgh to the one of the county's most significant monastic institutions. It also goes some way towards explaining the scale and quality of the workmanship exhibited in the parish church. Wymondham priory was founded in 1107 by William d'Aubigny (often Latinised as d'Albini), the Royal Butler to Henry I and a major landholder in Norfolk. The foundation charter established Wymondham as a daughter house – or priory – of the Benedictine abbey of St Albans and d'Aubigny endowed his new foundation with land, churches, tithes and rents (Page 1906, 336–43).

In addition to granting him estates, Henry I also arranged for William d'Aubigny to marry Maud Bigod, the daughter and heiress of Roger Bigod, the first Earl of Norfolk and a major East Anglian landholder. After Roger Bigod's death in 1107 Maud had become a royal ward and the Bigod estates had been placed under royal control, perhaps making the arrangement of this marriage easier. Happisburgh was among Bigod's landholdings at the time of his death and ownership of the estate was given to William d'Aubigny as a part of Maud's dowry.

Maud died in childbirth in the mid-1120s and both she and the baby seem to have been buried at Wymondham priory, rather than at Happisburgh, as some sources have suggested. To mark their burial, d'Aubigny granted the manor

The ruins of Wymondham Abbey viewed from the air in June 1989. The fields in the foreground contain the buried remains of the monastic buildings which stood in the abbey precinct. (© Norfolk County Council, photographed by D.A. Edwards: TG1001/AD2/DHU10)

of Happisburgh to the priory and confirmed the donation by offering on the high altar a silver cross containing many relics, including a fragment of the true cross (Shopland 2007, 17–20). This was the beginning of a relationship between the monks of Wymondham and the parishioners of Happisburgh which was to last for some 400 years until the middle of the 16th century.

The main source of income from monastic estates such as Happisburgh was grain, although monasteries such as Wymondham also had interests in other enterprises such as mills, salt pans and eel fishing, as well as the rights to wrecks off the coast. Wymondham's monastic accounts for the year 1395 indicate that the total income for the priory was £450, of which £134 was derived from renting out farm land and collecting manorial dues from the monastic estate at Happisburgh. The Happisburgh estate is also recorded as having provided rabbits for the monks' dining table. By 1444 and 1445 the money-collecting system had been simplified

This photograph shows rabbits being harvested at Hill Farm in 1937. According to monastic accounts, during the medieval period Happisburgh provided rabbits for the dining table of the monks of Wymondham Abbey.

and the estate at Happisburgh was being farmed out for a fixed rent of about £90 per year (Cattermole 2007a, 50–2, 55).

In addition to acquiring the Happisburgh estate, the priory also appropriated Happisburgh church, giving them the right to the tithes from the village. With ownership of the rectory estate came the responsibility for maintaining the fabric of the chancel, and it is likely that the surviving chancel of Happisburgh church was built at the expense of Wymondham priory. It would also appear that Wymondham stonemasons had an influence on the design of these buildings and there are a number of architectural features which bear their distinctive style. At Happisburgh, there are similarities between the moulding and hanging shields which surround the church's western doorway and the windows of the nave clerestory at Wymondham (Cattermole 2007b, 58–9). The design of the church font is also reminiscent of the font at Wymondham.

The western doorway of Happisburgh church, said to have similarities with architectural devices employed at Wymondham.

While for the most part the relationship between Wymondham and Happisburgh seems to have been relatively peaceful and prosperous, there are records of times during which tensions rose between the two parties. For example, shortly after the appointment of Ralph de Miers as prior of Wymondham in 1160 the tenants of Happisburgh refused to pay the dues and services which they owed to the priory. This dispute caused Ralph and a retinue of servants drawn from the priory and from d'Aubigny's son's household, to travel to Happisburgh where they broke down the tenants' doors and took their

owed goods by force. The Happisburgh tenants in their turn took their case to the Abbot of St Albans, who ultimately had jurisdiction over Wymondham, and he in turn asserted his authority over the priory (Page 1906, 43).

On 22 August 1537 the last abbot of Wymondham, Abbot Loys (Eligius), wrote to Thomas Cromwell acknowledging the receipt of a letter requiring them to grant a lease of the manor of Happisburgh to one William Clifton, but stating that they were reluctant to do so because of the benefits which the estate had for the abbey. Loy's letter also stated that the Happisburgh estate had never been let and that it provided valuable resources in the form of fish and rights over wrecks, as well as grazing land for the sheep which the abbey relied upon when providing food for guests (Page 1906, 342).

Cromwell's reply is not recorded, but from the second letter which Abbot Loys wrote to him on 13 September 1537 it is clear that Cromwell had disputed their claims that Happisburgh had never been let and that the ability of the abbey to provide hospitality would be affected by the loss of grazing land. The abbot in turn clarified that some, but not all of the abbey's Happisburgh holdings had been leased in the past, and claimed that should the Happisburgh lands be leased it would be necessary for the sheep to be sold and the abbey to begin buying its meat from the market instead (Page 1906, 342). These protests clearly fell on deaf ears and a third letter written to Cromwell on 30 January 1538 stated that on his return from London, Loys had told the other monks of Wymondham of Cromwell's 'great goodness' and referred to 'sinister and untrue reports' of the abbot which had been made by William Clifton, presumably by then the tenant of the Happisburgh estate (Page 1906, 342).

Aside from the church, which is considered at length in the next chapter, there are very few medieval buildings surviving in Happisburgh, although there are a couple of buildings which have potential links to the monastic community at Wymondham. The first is Tithe Barn, a flint and thatch building not far from the church, which is suggested locally to have been the barn

Tithe Barn in the 1970s, before its conversion to a residential property. Suggested locally to have been the barn from which the monks of Wymondham collected their tithes.

to which the monks of Wymondham may have paid a yearly visit to collect their tithes, although there is little architectural evidence to support this suggestion. The second building is the thatched flint and brick house known as the Monastery, which stands on the corner of the main street through the village, just to the south-west of the Hill House. The Monastery is an L-shaped house, the eastern range of which represents the remains of a 15th-century open-hall house, that is, a house in which the interior was open to the roof for some or all of its length. A buttery and a pantry would have existed at one end, with a cross-passage corridor linking the front and back doors of the hall. A substantial, and contemporary, brick fireplace apparently stood at the opposite end of the hall. It seems likely that the upper floor was probably inserted into the hall in the 18th century, at the point at which the roof was rebuilt. One of the ground-floor rooms in the eastern range has a brick piscina built into its wall, which is very unusual, as these are usually only found in churches or chapels, adding weight to the supposed ecclesi-

astical connections. Ultimately, although there is no definite proof that this house did belong to the monks of Wymondham, it is certainly a very interesting property and a particularly early survival in the Happisburgh area (NHER 12471; Pevsner and Wilson 1997, 540).

The two thatched houses to the right of the frame were once a row of six cottages. The Monastery – the house on the right – is so called because it is thought that the monks of Wymondham may have used it when collecting tithes from their Happisburgh estate. The adjoining house is Thrums. The Post Office and General Stores to the left of the frame was demolished in the early 1960s and the Post Office returned to the Wayside Stores.

Chapter 5

Happisburgh Church and Clergy

Although the presence of a church in Happisburgh was not explicitly recorded in the Domesday survey of 1086, as we have seen, it is very likely that a church stood on or near to the site of the present church during the Anglo-Saxon period. By the eleventh century many of the parish churches which we know today had been founded, and given Happisburgh's likely status as the head manor of the Happing Hundred during the Anglo-Saxon period it would be unusual for there not to have been a church at Happisburgh. As is the case with most of the known examples of Anglo-Saxon churches in the Eastern region, the earliest church on the site is likely to have been built of wood, only later being rebuilt in stone during the aftermath of the Norman Conquest. Indeed, traces of Norman architectural stonework have been claimed to have been identified reworked into the tower at Happisburgh, perhaps indicating that a Norman stone church was dismantled and its materials reused.

The Building

This section is based on notes made by Edwin Rose, formerly of the Norfolk Historic Environment Service, held by the Norfolk Historic Environment Record (NHER 7091).

Dedicated to St Mary, Happisburgh church is set on a rise above the village centre, from which its impressive and commanding tower can be seen for miles around (NHER 7091). Much of the visible fabric of the church, including the tower, is constructed in the 15th-century Perpendicular Gothic style, indicating a large-scale rebuilding at this time, although there are also surviving traces of 14th-century Decorated Gothic

The imposing western tower of Happisburgh church in 2010.

features, suggesting that at least one major phase of reconstruction had occurred previously.

The tower is some 110 feet tall, with striking battlements, making it one of the tallest, and finest, examples in the county. The tower's diagonal corner buttresses rise to the very top of the tower and, as was referred to in the previous chapter, there is a western doorway with a flint flushwork surround and carved spandrels, set below a 15th-century west window. A doorway in the internal south-eastern corner of the nave leads to a stone staircase up the inside of the tower, and there are small windows in the stair-well and a spyhole to the nave. From the stairs, a doorway leads to a first-floor ringing gallery, but for a long time the doorway was blocked by bricks, the gallery having been removed; this was reinstated late in 2010 and kitchen and toilet facilities inserted beneath it.

The floor above – known as the silence chamber – is also entered by a doorway from the stairs and on the exterior eastern face of the tower, above the nave roof and off-centred to the south, is a crude round-headed doorway, possibly the Norman stonework in the tower referred to above. This doorway opened above the line of the nave roof as far back as 1824, when Ladbrooke's print was made, but may once have been located below the roof level to provide access to a roof-space.

The third stage of the tower has intricate stone grilles forming rectangular soundholes, each with quoins of medieval brick. This level

The tower arch in 2011, showing the new ringing gallery installed in 2010 and the large western window. Note the misalignment between the nave and the tower, which it would seem were mistakenly laid out on slightly different alignments.

Ladbrooke's drawing of Happisburgh church from the south-east in 1824. Ladbrooke drew many of Norfolk's churches and his work provides a valuable early record, but we must be wary of the potential for the use of artistic licence. (Image courtesy of Norfolk County Council Library and Information Service)

An interior view of Happisburgh church showing the nave arcades, taken in the early years of the 20th century before the installation of electric lights.

now houses the bells, four in a row and two to one side in a wooden frame held together by iron ties, and with crossing braces in each side forming a row of Xs. The bell frame does not appear to be of very great age, and may only be 19th century, although it might incorporate older parts, and the bells themselves are discussed further below.

The nave and aisles are built of pebble flint, with knapped flint only presented on the south wall, it often being the case that the quality of the finish on the main approach to the church is higher than on the 'back' of the church. The north and south arcades and the chancel arch are also 15th-century Perpendicular, but the eastern respond of a 14th-century Decorated arcade survives because it supports the rood stair to the north of the chancel arch, indicating the replacement of an early set of arcades.

The font dates from the 15th century, but was recut during restoration work in the 19th century. The stem is surrounded by 'wild men' or 'woodwoses' and lions. The symbols of the four evangelists are carved on the bowl: a man for St Matthew, a lion for St Mark, an ox for St Luke and an eagle for St John. These carvings alternate with angels playing stringed instru-

ments. Unlike many fonts of this type, the four wild men carrying clubs and the four lions surrounding the stem are set under canopies.

The western wall of the south aisle and porch, which exhibits signs of a now demolished building which stood in the angle of the tower and the aisle.

There is architectural evidence to suggest that some sort of building has been demolished at the western end of the southern aisle. A blocked lancet window survives in the aisle wall below its roofline, where its relationship with the Perpendicular window suggests that this building survived until at least the 15th century. It has been suggested that this may have been an anchorite's cell or a small chapel, although there is nothing in the documentary history of the church which sheds any light on this.

There is a cusped piscina at the eastern end of the south aisle, and a recess in the southern wall. Ladbrooke's print shows both the east window of the southern aisle and the easternmost window in the southern wall in their present Perpendicular style, but he clearly depicts the other three windows in the south wall as having wooden tracery. These windows are now all in the Perpendicular style, presumably having been re-made during the 19th-century restoration of the building.

There are four southern buttresses, placed between the windows, and two angle buttresses; one buttress is overlain by the eastern wall of the porch, indicating that it predates the porch's construction. The north aisle has similar windows, but here alternate buttresses have been repaired in later brickwork. There are flint flushwork battlements on both nave and aisles, complementing those of the tower, and there is a Perpendicular clerestory. Somewhat unusually,

this contains an east window, although this would seem to be a Victorian insertion, as Ladbrooke shows a much smaller and higher opening.

The chancel is of poorer quality flintwork than the nave and aisles, with much random brick in the eastern wall, and lumps of iron-bound conglomerate in the east end of the southern wall. In the northern wall of the chancel is a blocked clerestory of two windows of double lancets under a straight head, and below these are two large blocked windows with much brick in the blocking. At the eastern end of this wall is a triangular-headed doorway in an unusual position. The lack of other openings suggests that there may have been a vestry here, the clerestory looking out above its roof, and the large windows must date from after its destruction. In the southern wall of the chancel, by contrast, are two large blocked arches, the eastern of which is set slightly higher. Ladbrooke did not show these arches, but did depict a partly blocked three-light window in the blocking of the eastern arch and

The northern wall of the chancel, showing the blocked windows of the clerestory and larger blocked windows beneath. The slight remains of a triangular-headed door can just be made out at the eastern end of this wall.

a two-light straight-headed Perpendicular window in the western arch. Above each was a clerestory window identical to those in the northern wall. These clerestory windows have now gone, and the windows in the arch blockings have been replaced with large Victorian windows in the Decorated style which cut the arches. The southern wall is divided by a buttress beside which is a little pointed priest's door. The eastern wall has angle buttresses and a Perpendicular window, the stained glass of which was installed in 1912. Although many of the windows in the chancel are 15th century, there is a 14th-century piscina inside the chancel indicating its earlier construction date. The triptych mounted in front of this window was given by Miss Diana Cator in 1925.

THE ALTAR, ST. MARY'S CHURCH. HAPPISBURGH

A view of the altar in the early 20th century, showing the triptych given by Miss Diana Cator in 1925.

The entrance to the south porch is spandrelled and the porch has windows to the east and west. Inside, an ornate piscina is supported on a head corbel. There is a fine ribbed wooden ceiling with a central carved boss. The porch has an upper storey, the stair for which rises from a door inside the nave, and this storey has slit windows to each side. Above the entrance arch is a two-light window, with a niche between the lights containing a statue stated in the church guide to be a copy of a 15th-century original destroyed in World War II, although Ladbrooke shows a different window here, with no niche and no statue. The flushwork battlements of the aisle continue onto the porch.

In summary, the present church is largely of 14th-century construction. A fragment of a north arcade remains, and evidence of a building against the south aisle west wall, showing that there were two aisles at this time. There seems to have been a south chapel to the chancel, and a north vestry, with a clerestory above each. The south porch overlies one buttress, indicating that the buttresses at least are pre-15th century. In the 15th century a thorough rebuilding took place with new tower, arcades, windows and porch. The two large windows in the north wall of the chancel suggest that the vestry had gone by this time; Ladbrooke's depiction of the windows in the southern wall is not clear enough to be certain, but these could be 15th century, and presumably the buttress and priest's door post-date the chapel's destruction. As was usual, decay ensued in the 18th century, shown by the blocked windows and those replaced in wood. As is described further below, a fire occurred in 1821 and restoration continued until 1860. The church was also bombed and substantially damaged during the Second World War, the effects of which are described in a later chapter.

The Bells
In the early 15th century there were only three bells installed, and according to the inventory which was taken of the building in 1552, the Royal Commissioners took the two largest away. These bells must have been replaced, as in 1637

there were again three bells, weighing approximately 8, 10 and 14 cwts. In that year the bells were recast by John Brend at his All Saints' Green foundry in Norwich and two more bells were added to make a ring of five, with the tenor weighing 11 cwt. Two of these 17th-century bells are still in the tower and both bear the inscription 'John Brend made me 1637' (Cattermole 1990, 28–9, 186–8).

In 1924, the Fourth and the Tenor bells were again recast and a new Treble was given by Mrs Mary Cator in memory of the Nelson's men of *HMS Invincible* who were wrecked off Happisburgh in 1801. During this restoration, the bells were brought down to a lower level in the tower, and the whole restoration was undertaken as an act of memorial to the men of the Royal Navy and Merchantile Marine who had lost their lives in the First World War.

On the recast Tenor bell is inscribed the following verse:

> To those who never turned their backs but
> Marched breast forward, never doubted
> clouds would break.
>
> Never dreamed though right were worsted,
> wrong would triumph.
> Held, we fall to rise, are baffled to fight
> better, sleep to wake.

On 15 April 1924 the *Eastern Daily Press* reported: 'On Saturday afternoon the Bishop of Norwich will dedicate the bells of St Mary's, Happisburgh, which have been silent for more than a century. The secretary of the Norfolk Guild of Ringers has arranged to bring a team of ringers for the occasion. … Mr Percy Pinkerton of Happisburgh has written a poem on the restored bells, which has been set to music by Mr H.A. Donald (London) and it will be sung by the choir on the day of dedication.'

The bells were removed again in November 1975. Owing to a crack in the crown, the Second bell was recast by Taylors of Loughborough and it now bears the inscription:

J.E. Large	Vicar
B.E. Trett	
E.A. Bennington	} Churchwardens
G.E. Larter	Captain of the Ringers

To the Glory of God
this Bell was recast
and the Peal rehung 1976

The other bells were retuned; the Third and Fifth one-eighth turned and the Fourth and Tenor one-quarter turned. All of the bells were rehung on new metal headstocks and ball-bearings, and given new rope pulley blocks. The bells were rededicated by the Bishop of

The rehanging of the tower's Second bell after it was recast in 1976.

Thetford at the Patronal Festival Evensong on 3 July 1977.

In June 1985, two new Treble bells from redundant churches were installed and dedicated by the Very Reverend Gilbert Thurlow, Dean Emeritus of Gloucester. The inscriptions on these two bells read:

Maria Stella Maris: Succurre piissima nobis
Vicar Reverend N. Martin
Recast 1985 from St Martin at Palace

and

Ad Gloriam Dei
Churchwardens E. Lovett, H. Mason
Bell Captain G. Larter
Recast 1985 from Wood Dalling

A chiming bell was given to the church and was installed during the autumn of 1987 in an A-frame. It weighs about 5 cwt and was transferred from the disused church at Illington. This bell was cast by the Thetford bell-founder Thomas Draper and bears the inscription 'PRAYS GOD THOMAS DRAPER ME FECIT 1577' (Cattermole 1990, 204–5).

The Vicars of Happisburgh

The list of vicars of Happisburgh, as recorded on the board which hangs in the church, gives a complete sequence of incumbents from the 13th century onwards.

1266	Nicholas
1304	Robert de Henney
1307	Robert de Seyntefoy
1318	Henry de Masseworth
1331	Walter de Tyveteshale
1333	Walter Speller
1337	Simon de Banyngham
1355	Robert de Burghwode
1359	Hugh Smith
1361	John Waleys
1400	William Wimpewell
1416	Richard Sterre
1429	John Salle
1455	Thomas Nynyght
1491	Nicholas Nark
1496	Jeffrey Turnour
1527	John Dry S.T.B.
1536	William Syleham
1591	John Bird
1602	Richard Burrage
1638	William Eaton
1639	Thomas Bulbeck
1640	Nathaniel Vincent S.T.P.
1661	John Elwood
1667	John Elwood
1670	Henry Gooch
1688	Richard Kippingham
1692	William Harley
1706	Jonathan Chaloner
1727	Edmund Ludlow
1759	Roger Donne
1773	Theophilus Rice
1775	Robert Parr
1781	Thomas Lloyd
1814	Charles Prowett
1830	Charles Birch
1853	Richard Holmes
1859	James Slater
1895	Robert Aldous Hitchcock
1920	Joseph Patrick Quigly
1928	Cyril Deane
1942	George Mellor
1951	Joseph Denis Fox
1954	Cyril Matthew Smith
1956	Harry Reginald Chisnell
1966	John Edward Large
1979	Derek Fennessey Coombes
1984	Nicholas Roger Martin
1991	John Anthony Lines
1997	Richard Arthur Hines
2008	Philip Norman Wood

Reverend Theophilus Rice (1724–75)

The Reverend Theophilus Rice, vicar of Happisburgh, was baptized and buried in the village. He was educated at private schools in Oulton and Soham and at Caius College, Cambridge. Ordained deacon at Norwich in 1747 and priest in 1752, he was licensed curate of Lessingham, of Brumstead and, in 1770, of

Happisburgh. He was vicar of the parish and rector of Eccles from 1773 until his death. Among his many bequests, he left the house bought by his father (now known as Seacroft) to Robert Bartram, the son of his stepsister. Five guineas were left to Martha Crosskill, 'upon account of her very dutiful behaviour to my father whilst she kept house for him and for me'. Two shillings and sixpence were left to Robert Betts, the parish clerk, and half a guinea to 'John, son of John Thompson upon Happisburgh Hill'. James Faulke received his 'silver watch with the china dial plate', while John Wells, clerk, received his gown, cassock and sash. All of the volumes of the *Spectator*, the *Guardian* and *Tatler* in Rice's possession were given to Robert Summers, the schoolmaster. Finally, five pounds were to be divided among the poor people of Happisburgh.

Reverend James Slater (1816–1895)

When the Reverend James Slater brought his wife and daughter to Happisburgh in 1859 he found the newly built vicarage in sharp contrast to the church, which was in a pitiful state. Thirty-seven years earlier, a large wooden cross on top of the tower had been struck by lightning, which, together with a portion of the tower, fell on the roofs below causing a fire. The tower was repaired, but the nave and south aisle were left open to the weather. Services were held in the chancel. The new Vicar set about planning a complete restoration: new roofs throughout; all windows renovated and re-glazed (many had been blocked by brickwork); box pews replaced by open benches; the tower gallery removed; the font cleansed of paint, re-cut and placed on two steps; and the floor repaved with local tiles. Slater also had the floor raised by the addition of steps between the west end, the chancel and the sanctuary. Wall monuments, with the exception of those to two earlier vicars, were removed and placed under the new flooring.

As the *Eastern Daily Press* recorded in 1864:

'Thursday, June 9th, was an auspicious day for the inhabitants of this sea-side village, as being marked by

A 19th-century portrait of the Reverend James Slater which now hangs in the Church Rooms.

an event ever to be remembered by themselves and their children with feelings of thankfulness and joy – the re-opening of their fine old parish church. … It cannot but afford the highest satisfaction to the vicar and his parishioners and friends who have so heartily co-operated in this work of faith and labour of love.

'The Lord Bishop of the Diocese, and about seventy of the clergy and neighbouring gentry assembled at the vicarage on the day in question, and then partook of luncheon, which was served in the school-room at half past one o'clock. The room was tastefully decorated for the occasion, and presented a very pleasing appearance.

'After luncheon, the clergy accompanied the bishop to the church, and the procession was met at the gate by the churchwardens, who conducted his lordship and the clergy to their seats in

A view of the Old Vicarage taken c.1910. The vicarage was built in 1860 and the Reverend James Slater and his family were the first inhabitants. The new vicarage – now The Rectory – was built in 1978.

the chancel. The Rev J. Gunn, rural dean and rector of Irstead and Barton, acted as chaplain to the bishop. The church was full to overflowing; and not withstanding its spacious area and extensive seat-accommodation, it proved insufficient for the assembled congregation, about 200 of whom were obliged to remain outside, being unable to obtain admittance.

'Evening prayer was said at three o'clock. ... A most appropriate and impressive sermon was preached by the Bishop, from St Luke 7:5, 'He loveth our nation and hath built us a synagogue.' The choirs of several adjacent parishes kindly attended, and lent their valuable aid to the Happisburgh choir, in conducting the musical part of the service.

'The farmers, almost without exception, gave their labourers a half-holiday to afford them an opportunity of attending the church, and the day being kept as a festive day throughout the parish, will ever be looked back upon with unmixed pleasure by all who shared in its proceedings.'

High praise, indeed, but the restoration did not meet with everyone's approval. Walter Rye,

in his *A History of Norfolk* (1885), wrote of the church that it

> 'was still a very fine one, though it was most shamefully 'restored' in 1863, every monument but one in the church (it is said that there were hundreds of them) having been covered up by the new tiling – an act of vandalism which I venture to think is unparalleled in the whole county, and one which would not be ventured upon by the most impudent parson of the present generation. The tower has luckily escaped the attentions of the architect and his employer; indeed, it would have been hard for them to have found an excuse to lay hands on so perfect an erection' (Rye 1885, 245–6)

Great as his interest was in the church building, Mr Slater was more concerned with the welfare of his flock, and spent much time visiting his parishioners. His wife and daughter provided soup for the sick, including school children suffering from whooping cough, and during an epidemic of scarlet fever distributed leaflets to all the children on 'the containing of the disease'. Mr Slater went into school at least twice a week to teach scripture and arithmetic, and was always ready to give help and advice when needed. Mrs Slater supervised the girls' needlework, and Miss Eliza Slater taught singing. In preparation for celebrating the Queen's Jubilee in 1887 she practised the National Anthem and other suitable songs with the children. In an emergency the Vicarage family took charge of the whole school.

In 1887, Walcott was united with Happisburgh for ecclesiastical purposes, and so Mr Slater's last years were spent as vicar of both parishes. Mr Slater and his family were much loved and respected by the parishioners. There was great sorrow when he died on 12 May 1895. The following account of his funeral is from the *Eastern Daily Press*:

'Amid feelings of profound regret the interment of the venerable and venerated vicar of Happisburgh, the Rev. James Slater, took place at noon on Thursday. The coffin was borne by six of the villagers. ... The scene in church was most impressive. The spacious and beautiful building, a lasting monument of their departed pastor's zeal and loving care was filled ... with sorrowing parishioners. In the solemn pauses of the service the rushing of the wind and the roar of the sea sounded like a mournful requiem.'

Mr Slater's only surviving close family member was his son, Lieutenant Colonel James Barry Slater, late 2nd Sikh Regiment, who erected a large brass memorial tablet on the north wall of the church, commemorating his father, mother and sister. The village's tribute was to build the Slater Memorial Church Room in memory of their beloved vicar. Today, enlarged and refurbished, it stands next to the Old Vicarage and not far from the church. Within hangs a portrait of the Reverend James Slater, his benign and friendly face looked up to by future generations of parishioners.

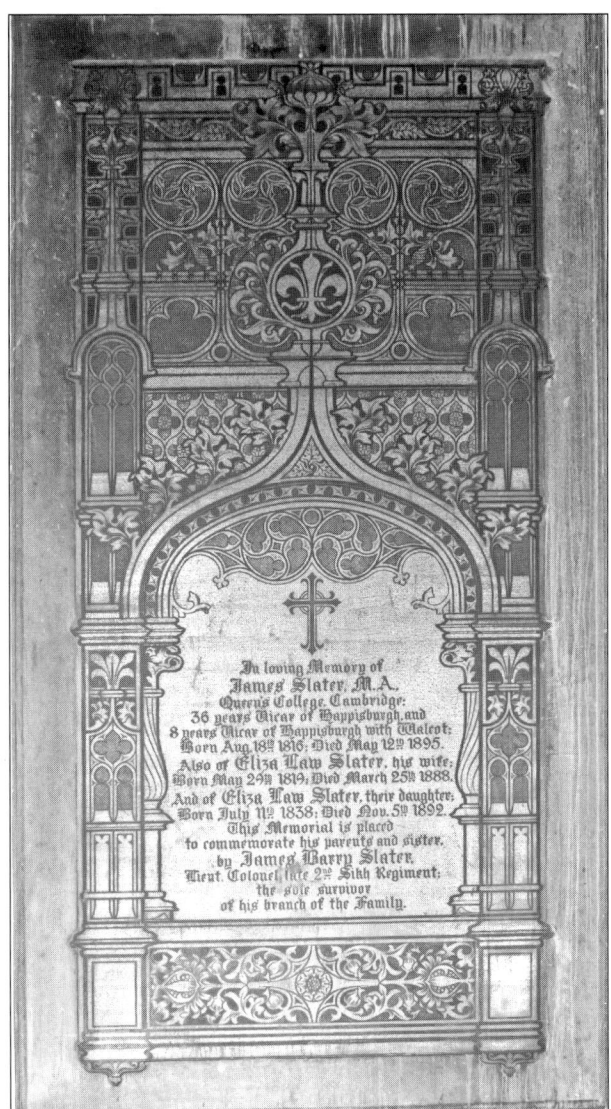

The memorial brass to the Reverend James Slater, erected by his son, Lieutenant Colonel James Barry Slater, on the north wall of the church.

The Reverend Cyril Deane (seated, centre) and his wife (seated, left) moved from Tunstead to Happisburgh Vicarage with their children Margaret (right), Winifred (left) and Alan (centre). Their maid, Ivy Pestell (back, left), came with them and spent the rest of her life in the village.

The Church Rooms, built as a memorial to the Reverend James Slater, and still much used for village events.

Residents of Happisburgh gather in the vicarage garden to celebrate the 25th wedding anniversary of the Reverend and Mrs Hitchcock on 4th June 1910.

The Reverend J.D. Fox, his churchwardens and sidesmen in the early 1950s. Left to right: Fred Mowle, Bert Larter, B.E. Trett, John Weddall, Reverend Fox, Jack Spanton, Duncan Fletcher, William French, Tom Dobson.

The Reverend Harry Chisnell came to the village with his wife Diana. Catherine was born a few years later, and was the first baby to live in the Vicarage. She was followed by her brother Paul.

The Reverend J.E. Large had been a missionary in Namibia, but returned to England due to ill health. In 1977, the parishes of Hempstead with Eccles and Lessingham became part of his incumbency and at about the same time he moved into the new Vicarage built in the grounds of the old one.

The Reverend Dr Richard Hines became the first Rector of the benefice, now known as the Coastal Group of Parishes, which was increased in size by the addition of Bacton, Ridlington and Witton in 2005. Richard's wife Jen took a very active part in Church and village life, with a special interest in working with young people. After ten years they left the Coastal Group and Richard became Rector of the Falkland Islands, a far-flung parish extending to South Georgia.

The Reverend Nicholas Martin brought his wife Zillah and two small children to the parish. They were a very musical family, Nicholas playing the organ and piano, Zillah and Rachel the flute, and Christopher the trombone when still a very small boy. He is shown here with the choir: front row (l–r) Ivy Culum, Ivy Risborough, Daisy Neave, Betty Bane; second row (l–r) Ethel Hannant, Mary Oliver; back row (l–r) George Risborough, Philip Larter, James Butler, Duncan Larter, Gilbert Larter.

The Reverend Phil Wood and his wife Yvonne moved into the Rectory and faced the task of caring for nine parishes and eight medieval churches. He is ably assisted by the Reverend Eiler Mellerup and three Readers, Ray Sanders, Pam Millsted and Geoff Smith.

The Reverend Eiler Mellerup, retired Locally Ordained Minister.

The Church, Happisburgh.

A view of parishioners going to church taken as some point before the First World War. The woman in the foreground is the postmistress, Mrs F. Ducker. The wooden shed to the right of the frame, adjoining Camberley Cottage, was used as a butcher's shop for many years.

Ernest Watling shown sharpening his scythe during the mowing of the churchyard.

Ernest Watling (1926–2002)

Ernie, who was born at Swanton Abbot, moved to Happisburgh with his family when he was fourteen years old. For most of his life Ernie worked on the land, and for many years Saturday mornings were spent tidying the churchyard, in which he took a great pride. Before the general use of strimmers and power-driven cutters, the grass was scythed annually. Local farmers offered help and Ernie always joined in. Scything is skilled work and the technique is often passed down from father to son. From time to time, Ernie was asked to mark the position for a new grave. Although not proficient in reading or writing, he had an excellent memory, and knew the names of the occupants of the unmarked graves long after most people had forgotten.

He was a sidesman, and on Sunday mornings always sat in the corner seat of the back pew so that he could hand out books to late-comers and be ready to open the heavy door at the end of the service. When the sermon had gone on for ten minutes or so, Ernie would look at his watch, a gesture not unobserved by the Rector!

One of the highlights of Ernie's life was on Maundy Thursday 1977 when he received the Royal Maundy Money from the Queen in Norwich Cathedral in recognition of his devoted service to St Mary's church. Ernie was the only person from the village ever to receive that honour. Those silver coins were very greatly treasured.

Many of us still think of that seat in the back pew as being Ernie's and he is still much missed.

Chapter 6

Happisburgh in the 16th–18th Centuries

Little remains today of 16th-century Happisburgh, apart from the church. It dominated the village then, as now, but stood more than twice as far from the sea and was encircled by farmland and common. A cart track, now the main street, ran between the great open fields. Hedges were few, but formed part of the boundary between Walcott and East Ruston. At its low-lying southern end, where the parish adjoined Lessingham, there was marshland and common. As they do today, North Sea gales stunted and distorted the trees, which then formed a wood to the north-west of the village. The strips in the open fields were farmed by a great number of people; the strips of the yeomen who owned their land being interspersed with those of the shoemaker, blacksmith, publican and many others who held land on a variety of tenures, as well as the priest's glebe, from which he obtained a part of his income.

This chapter tells some of the stories of the individuals and families which made up Happisburgh's population during the 16th to 18th centuries.

Many aspects of the family histories and daily lives of Happisburgh's residents can be reconstructed from the documentary evidence which they left behind, much of it administrative in nature. The parish records which provide a near-continuous list of the baptisms, marriages and burials in the parish from 1558 until the present day are a particularly rich source of information. With the exception of the current volumes, the originals of all of Happisburgh's baptism, marriage and burial registers are held by the Norfolk Record Office (NRO PD516) where copies of many of the registers are also available to view on microform or in transcription.

Wills provide another valuable source of information, both with regard to the wealth and possessions of an individual and with regard to the nature of their relationships with family and friends. Occasionally, additional bequests will be left to institutions and building or restoration projects, or provision made for the poor, or for the provision of a memorial to the deceased, all of which provide additional insights into the village and its inhabitants.

Another invaluable source are probate inventories, which provide a series of very detailed snapshots of individuals' households and possessions at the time of their deaths. Between 1530 and 1782 it was obligatory for the executor of a will to register an inventory of the nature and value of the deceased's goods with the local probate court; although such inventories continued to be made after 1782, they were no longer a requirement of the process. Probate inventories were compiled or 'apprised' by two or more of the deceased's neighbours who were considered to be competent and qualified to assess the value of the goods. The Norfolk Record Office holds details of a large number of wills and probate inventories from Happisburgh, and these have been used to illuminate the lives of the village's past residents.

Churchwardens

If Happisburgh ever possessed a manor house and resident lords of the manor, no trace of them remains. It was around the incumbent, assisted by his churchwardens, that the organisation of parish life developed. Twice a year, representatives of the principal village families met at the vestry meeting, and at Easter chose two of their number to take office as churchwarden. For at least 200 years, from 1530 to 1750, members of the Middleton, Chamberlyne, Harris and Callow families took an active part in the life of the village, often filling this post. Although not necessarily highly educated, some of their number could read and write.

The duties of the churchwarden were many and varied, ranging from attendance at the twice-yearly Visitation to 'present' whatever was amiss in the parish, to responsibility for the destruction of vermin. One of their more important duties, then as now, was to maintain the fabric of the church and care for all of its ornaments and possessions. As failure to perform their tasks could render them liable to excommunication, they were generally thorough in their work (Pounds 2000, 182–6). When Bishop Redman held his Visitation on Tuesday 22 November 1597, the churchwardens reported that the vicar, Cannan by name, had 'read the Queen's Injunctions but once these three quarters of a year'. They also cited Thomas Baxter 'for not comying to church'. Presumably Thomas had not asked for absolution at the Archdeacon's Court. The fine for non-attendance at church was one shilling, a very considerable sum (Williams 1946).

John Callowe was churchwarden at a most difficult period in the life of the village, and indeed of England. When he took office in 1552, the living had been vacant and unserved for ten years, so that in all probability the *English Prayer Book* (which should have replaced the Latin missal in 1549) had never been used. However, on the morning of 2 September 1552, six Royal Commissioners sent by the Privy Council of the 15-year-old Edward VI arrived. They summoned John and his fellow churchwarden Robert Elwin, and in their presence drew up an inventory of the church's possessions. The most precious of these were two gilt chalices and patens, a pair of silver censers, and the three bells in the tower. A copper cross valued at sixpence was also included, as were the velvet and satin copes and vestments (Walters 1952, 371–2).

Then, under the eyes of the two helpless men, the Commissioners rode off with all but the 'best chalis and the best bell'. It was little comfort to the churchwardens to hear that all over England churches were being robbed in that way because 'the Kinge's Majestie had neede presently of a masse of money'. Today, Happisburgh church still has the paten belonging to the 'best chalis'. The gilt has long since worn off, as has the enamel which once coloured the vernicle on the centre. Lovely as it is, how much John Callowe must have grieved for the loss of the even lovelier treasure in his care.

The Constable

During the reign of Mary, Roman Catholic rites returned and Latin was once again the language of the church, but in 1558 when Elizabeth succeeded to the throne, the people of Happisburgh, in common with the rest of the country, were ordered to revert to the *English Prayer Book*. It was in this same year that John Callowe married. He and his wife Margaret had six children, and although William, the eldest, died when little more than a week old, Gefreye grew up to carry on the family farm. He married Mary Chamberlyne, who also came from a yeoman family.

Mary's brother Thomas lived in a reasonably large farm house which was comfortably furnished. Amongst his treasured possessions, as highlighted in his probate inventory, was a bible, a looking glass and a silver cup. His well curtained four-poster bed was complete with a feather mattress, bolsters, pillow, blanket and coverlet (NRO DN/INV 47A/149). Thomas' son, also called Thomas Chamberlyne, in time took his turn in parish government as other members of his family had done before him. He was described on his death in 1670 as 'gent and cheife Cuntstable for this division' (NRO ANF, will register, 1670–71, fo.350, no.88). The post of parish constable was an important one; he had the power to arrest any who committed a crime or caused a breach of the peace, and could hold the culprit in the stocks or in custody until a magistrate's court assembled (Pounds 2000, 193–5).

Vagrants were regarded as criminals who were to be whipped and sent back to the place from whence they had come. It was the constable who administered the punishment and passed the poor creature on to the constable of the next parish with a pass obtained from a magistrate. As each village was responsible for its own poor, no one was anxious to support the wanderer, and every effort was made to get rid of him as quickly and easily as possible. To this end, and although against the law, magistrates sometimes gave passes to vagrants without previous punishment. This was the custom in Happisburgh for some years before Thomas Chamberlyne's term of office began, as is shown by the following entry in the parish register:

> 'Matthewe Benstead of Wretton in the county of Norff. and Alice his wife was taken vagrant at Happesburgh on 19th day of November 1630 and had assigned them for their return home 5 days.'

Five years later, John Bird of Kee in Northampton with his wife and three small children were found homeless in the cold weather of February, and were allowed fifteen days to return from whence they had come.

If a stranger was staying temporarily in the village, as was often the case at harvest time, when extra help was needed, he had to bring a certificate from the incumbent of his own parish agreeing to take him back. Robert Stockdale of Tasburgh 'comenge to Hapsburgh as a harvest man' never made the return journey, for he was 'here buryed upon the 22 day of August 1664'.

No stranger was allowed to settle in a village unless he rented a property of at least £10 value or could show that he had sufficient to support himself. These qualifications evidently were fulfilled by William Pinn, 'a stranger comeing from Lopeingland in Suffolk being a husbandman' who was buried in Happisburgh churchyard on the last day of April 1671.

The primary duty of the constable was to take charge of the arrangements for keeping watch and ward in the parish. He was responsible for the parish armour, maintained the archery butts, took the men of the village to the musters which were required by law, and provided money for their maintenance. Many yeoman had their own armour and weapons. When Edmund Middleton died in 1598, 'one muskett and two calivers, one holbard and a coate of male' were found together with '10 combs of otes and a stone of wool' in the upper chamber of his house (NRO NCC, will register, Adams, 83).

John Gerard

An event took place on a wet Friday night in October 1588 which escaped the notice of the parish constable. A small boat put out from a French vessel anchored close to the shore and dropped two men on the beach at the northern end of the village. They were Jesuit priests, Father Edward Oldcorne and Father John Gerard, a young man recently ordained in Rome. The sailing of the Spanish fleet against England that summer had increased the feelings against Roman Catholicism and throughout the country close watch was being kept for recusants. After praying for guidance, the two men looked for a track leading away from the village, but each path they took in the darkness led to a house and barking dogs. At length they decided to wait until morning, spending the rest of the night in a nearby wood, which offered little shelter and no chance of sleep. At dawn they parted to make their separate ways to London: Father Oldcorne walked along the shore to

Mundesley, where he fell in with a party of sailors recently disbanded after the defeat of the Armada. Pretending to be one of their company, he travelled with them to London, eventually to suffer execution there for his faith.

John Gerard, on leaving the wood by another path, saw some Happisburgh folk approaching. Anxious not to arouse suspicion, he told them he was looking for his lost falcon. They listened sympathetically and were sorry they could not help. All day he walked away from the coast, avoiding public roads and villages. Wet and hungry, he risked spending the night at an inn, probably at Sloley. There he also bought a pony, for a stranger on foot might well be arrested as a vagrant. Next morning, as he approached Worstead, he rode straight into a group of men keeping watch for rogues and vagabonds. They insisted that he be taken to the Parish Constable and Officer of the Watch, who were in church attending morning prayer. At the long questioning which took place in the churchyard, John Gerard stuck to his story of the lost falcon and eventually was allowed to continue on his way. To avoid passing through the busiest streets of Norwich, he went around the city, entering by the Brayen Doors, which were then at the junction of Queen's Road and All Saints' Green.

After many dangers and hair's-breadth escapes while ministering his fellow recusants, Gerard was caught and imprisoned in the Tower of London. Torture failed to wring from him the names of his associates, and after his escape from the Tower he continued his work, always regretting that he had not been counted worthy to suffer martyrdom. We know so much about Gerard because he later wrote a Latin account of his life, which was eventually published in English translation as *The Autobiography of an Elizabethan* (Caraman 1951).

The Parish Register

The keeping of the register has been one of the duties of the parish priest since Thomas Cromwell, Lord Privy Seal to Henry VIII, issued Injunctions to this effect in 1538. All baptisms, marriages and burials had to be recorded on a Sunday in the presence of one of the wardens, on pain of a fine of 3s-4d to be applied to the repair of the church. Later, the fine was given to the poor men's box, and in the time of Queen Elizabeth was divided between the two causes. The register, which was to be kept in a two-lock coffer, often only consisted of loose sheets so that in 1597 the Convocation of Canterbury thought it necessary to direct that all entries be copied into books of parchment (Pounds 2000, 288–90).

In the next year, the vicar of Happisburgh sat down to his laborious task. He was no doubt the same man – Cannan – who had been reported by his churchwardens for failing to read the Queen's Injunctions, but the register was a duty which could not be ignored. Cannan's Christian name has been lost, and he does not appear in the official list of incumbents, but when the Reverend Richard Burrage was inducted into the living (with that of East Ruston) in 1602 he found the register in good order. At that time there were 195 communicants at Easter.

Richard Burrage, a Norfolk man ordained in Norwich two years earlier, had charge of the register for 36 years, during which time his entries included the baptisms of his own seven children. Neither he nor his predecessor bothered to sign each page, together with the wardens, as was required by law, but they did send a transcript to the archdeacon each year. Happisburgh was Richard Burrage's only cure, for he died in office early in January 1636 at the age of 63. In spite of this, it was in the nave of Salthouse church that he was buried, where a plain stone slab records that he was 'late preacher of God's Word at Happisburgh'. Unlike some clergy who were only allowed to read homilies, Burrage was licensed to preach.

Although the next two incumbents stayed but one year each, the register was well cared for by the curate John Boulte. He cut a wider nib than usual in his goose-feather quill to inscribe the year at the top of the pages and to enter the Christian names of the most important parishioners in larger letters. John, the son of Thomas and Anne Harris, was so favoured in his baptismal entry, for his father had been churchwarden two years previously. In that year, 1637, the three church bells had been recast at John Brend's Norwich foundry and two news bells purchased. The names of Thomas Harris and Thomas Hasted, his fellow churchwarden, were put upon them, as was the custom when any article was bought by the church, together with the inscription 'John Brend made me'. John Boulte was careful to note that the baptism of young John Harris had been 'by me John Boulte, clerke' and he also signed his name clearly at the foot of the page. By far the most important entry, in which all names are written in large letters, is the baptism on 19 September 1639 of 'ELIZA-BETH the daughter of JOHN BOULTE clearke and MARIE his wife'.

Not content with making the normal entries, Boulte also used his large nib to inscribe 'The Register Booke of Happesborrow' on the title page, and then translated a Latin rhyme 'When wedlock comes in and goe out':

> 'What ye Advent doth decree St
> Hillary doth set it free
> What Septuagena doth withstand
> the Eighth of Easter doth loose ye
> band
> What ye Rogation doth debarr the
> Trinity doth end the jarre'

The celebration of marriage was forbidden from Advent to the octave of the Epiphany from Septuagesima to the octave of Easter, and from the Sunday before Ascension Day to Trinity Sunday.

The Civil War appears to have made little impact on Happisburgh and its clergy, but during the Commonwealth an act of 1653 took from the ministers the custody of the registers and the right to celebrate marriages. A civil cere-mony was to be conducted by a justice of the peace and a 'Parish Register', elected by the ratepayers of the village and sworn before a magistrate, was given charge of the registers. He could collect a fee of one shilling for each birth and four pence for each burial he recorded.

In Happisburgh the choice fell on Henry Middleton, a well educated member of a res-pected yeoman family and contemporary of Thomas Chamberlyne. Henry's younger brother

George had been to Trinity Hall, Cambridge, a suitable choice for a Norfolk man, for its founder was Bishop Bateman of Norwich. After his ordination at Peterborough in 1615, George had served as curate at Happisburgh under Richard Burrage.

Henry kept the register in a small neat hand, and as a rule was conscientious and thorough. He noted the age against several of the burial entries (which was not the custom at the time) and often gave a woman's maiden name. Occasionally, he lacked the necessary informa-tion and was obliged to leave spaces, as he did when entering a birth in 1656: '— the — of Henry Pye and Dionis his wife was borne the — day of —'. As Dionis died in childbirth it may well be that her distraught widower omitted to visit the Parish Register. During the Com-monwealth, births, not baptisms, were recorded.

In the section of the register devoted to marriages are three entries showing that the ceremony was performed by John Reymes, the magistrate, in the presence of Henry Middleton. Major John Reymes of Overstrand was an ardent Puritan who served on the Parliamentary Committee for Norfolk. One of his duties, which he appears to have carried out with relish, was to eject those clergy who remained faithful to the Prayer Book and the tenets of Archbishop Laud. The family of Dr Thomas Reeve of Aldborough and Colby suffered at his hands when he brutally searched and ransacked their vicarage. Fortunately, the Doctor, for whom Reymes had a warrant, escaped arrest, but his wife and six children were turned out of the house. Reyme's signature, together with that of the Parish Register, appears at the end of the following entry:

'An° 1654

Henry Parr gent and Miss Muriall Armiger were married the 4th day of May in the yeare aforesaid by John Reymes Esq. and upon the Tuesday next after were married by a lawful Minister in Hapsburgh Church.'

The 'lawful minister' was presumably Nathaniel Vincent, a Cornishman, and for some years a fellow of King's College Cambridge. He must, at the least, have accepted the Puritanical reforms outwardly, for he was the incumbent during the Civil War and remained so through-out the years of the Commonwealth.

In spite of the law, at least two marriages were solemnised by the curate, John Corye, in 1657 and are entered in a hand which is not Henry's. They are followed by the phrase: 'Cromwell his law is out'. The Reverend John Corye must also have been puritanical in his outlook and unable to adjust to the views of the Restoration and the new Prayer Book, for in 1662 he left the ministry to spend the next 36 years as a schoolmaster. His tombstone was in the burial ground of the Independents' Meeting House in Colegate, Norwich. Vincent's successor, John Elwood, the son of a Cumberland farmer, was no doubt in sympathy with Corye's opinions, for when he was instituted vicar in union with East Ruston in 1667 'he took not ye oath of canonicall obedience'.

Henry Middleton's entries of burials begin with a single carefully written inscription on an otherwise blank page:

> 'Rebeccah Middleton was buryed on the 3 of November 1652 beinge the daughter of Henry Middleton gt. and the said Rebeccah was 22 years of adge and upwards.'

Rebeccah was the youngest of Henry's four daughters – he had no sons. When Dorothy, the eldest girl, was 28 she met Edmund Rice, an Irishman who had settled recently in Norfolk. He came from a good family and when the two were married the match had Henry's blessing. Dorothy bore three sons, Theophilus, Henry and Edmund, but when young Edmund was only six years old the Parish Register made the following entry:

> 'Edmund Rice an Irish man who married Dorathie the daughter of Henry Middleton gent was buryed here the first day of July, and left an honest report behinde him of beinge an upright just and true dealing man, he being a man of 40 years of Adge or thereabouts who while he lived among us (beinge about 12 years) received such curteous use of the generality of good people as of wright belonged to a stranger for his loveinge and friendly behaviour. And whose Soule I trust resteth with the Lord. Written by Henry Middleton register and father of the said Dorathie.'

A tragic death recorded by Henry Middleton was that of Katherin Gase in 1657 who was 'burnt to dead upon 11th daye of September by the casual of her howse fallinge of ffier and burnt downe she beinge lame and not able to helpe her selfe and beinge then only alone in the howse at her age of 57 years or thereabouts'. Fires were not uncommon; in November that same year, Thomas Man's daughter Ann was also 'burnt to dead'.

Henry himself died in 1669 aged '80 years and noe more', but the will he surely must have made has not been found. However, William Middleton, a relation of his who died the next year left 'unto the poore of the Parrish of Happisburgh the sume of tenn shillings of lawfull money of England' to be paid within one month of his death. A hundred years earlier, in 1568 one Christopher Middleton left '12 pence to the poremens box', another 12 pence to the priest for 'tythes negligently forgotten', five shillings to the repair of the church and two shillings 'to the making of the bell' (NRO ANF, will register Liber 22 (Gottes), fo.247).

Henry must have been sorely missed in the parish. He kept the register until November 1666, six years after the end of the Commonwealth, and for a few months after his last entry there was much confusion. Baptisms and burials were recorded together by one unused to writing much. Then the entries were sorted out and rewritten in a careful hand. One points to an event which must have caused distress to the Callow family – the birth of William, 'base son of Mary Callow and of William Budd the reputed father'. William never married Mary, for two years later it is recorded that his wife Martha bore him a daughter whom they named Alice and in November the following year he died of smallpox.

Smallpox reappeared in the village from time to time. John Drake died of it in 1689, and three years later Hannah, the wife of John Turner, caught it and was buried in August. Just a week after this John was in church again for the funeral of his three-year-old daughter who had also fallen victim of the disease. At this time the use of a woollen shroud was required by law for all burials, except for those who had died of the plague. An Act of 1678, in an effort to promote the wool trade, demanded that 'no corpse … shall be buried in any shirt, shift, sheet or shroud or anything whatsoever made or mingled with flax, hemp, silk, hair, gold or silver, or in any stuff or thing, other than what is made of sheep's wool only' (Charles II, 1677 & 1678; Raithby 1819, 885–6).

In 1694, there were further impositions. The government levied a tax of two shillings for a birth, half a crown for a marriage and four shillings for a burial, with a sliding scale for the aristocracy, to obtain funds for 'carrying on the war against France with vigour'. It therefore became necessary for the priest to be notified of all births, whether the baby was baptised or not, for it was he who had to act as the tax collector. This custom persisted for a number of years after the tax was withdrawn, for on eight occasions between 1706 and 1721 Joseph Croskill

called at the vicarage to inform the Reverend Jonathan Challoner that his wife Hannah had given birth to yet another child, and to insist that the baby was not to be christened. One wonders what had occurred to change Joseph Craskill's mind, for the two eldest children had both been baptised.

The Middletons and the Chamberlins
Although Henry Middleton had no sons, the name of Middleton still appears frequently in the registers during the early years of the 18th century. Another Henry and William were serving from time to time as churchwardens, and when the church acquired a new oak chest in 1708 their names were chiselled roughly upon it:

W:H:MIDELTON:CHURCH:WAR:

No doubt the village carpenter, pressed for space, thought that the ampersand between the W and the H was unimportant. At the Bishop's Visitation the following year, when the two men were sworn in for a second term of office, they were also instructed to attend to the repair of a pillar in the church.

Henry had married Jane Chamberlain, grand-daughter of the one-time Chief Constable, Thomas Chamberlyne, in 1704, thereby linking two of the most important families in the parish. But Jane died two years later when their daughter Elizabeth was born – a sickly baby who lived for only a few months.

When Henry's father, Robert, died, the register entry gives him the title of 'gent' which was not, at that time, indiscriminately applied. In spite of this, the sum total of the old man's worldly goods at this death in 1713 amounted to only £12-5s-8d: 'his wearing apparell' and linen, ready money, 'one bed as it stands', 'one close stoole' and 'loose things not seen or forgotten' (NRO NCC, will register, Dawson, 312). Perhaps he had given his more valuable possessions to his son at an earlier date, and spent his last years as an invalid in Henry's house. The mention of a 'close stoole' or night commode, and the fact that the probate inventory was apprised by James' father point to this.

Poor as Robert Middleton appears to have been, many villagers, often with large families to support, had far less. Thomas Davy, a thatcher, had, it seems, little more than the bare essentials in his tiny cottage. One bed stood in the kitchen (or living room) and the other in the 'bakehouse' with only one pair sheets between them. The family cooking was done in the pottage pot or frying pan – there was no need to own a spit if one never had a joint to roast. At his death, the value of all of his possessions was estimated at £2-4s-0d, which included five shillings for 'the muck in the yard' (NRO DN/INV 74A/66). Little wonder that only one of his seven children survived infancy.

Village Tradesmen

Samuel Keeler, the village cordwainer, made a better living at his trade. His clifftop property had a room above the kitchen, the workshop in which he made boots, shoes and harnesses, a barn and sheds to house two cattle, his mare and a couple of pigs. When not busy with his leatherworking, Samuel's time was spent cultivating his land to provide corn for the family's bread, but in September 1709 he and his wife Jane had one fewer mouths to feed, for their ten-year-old daughter Sarah died. Just one year later, a seaman too near to death to give his name came ashore and was brought to Samuel's cottage. Efforts to revive the man failed, and on 20 September 1709 he too was buried in the churchyard. Perhaps he brought smallpox or some other disease with him, for three weeks later Samuel himself was dead.

After the funeral, Thomas Harley, churchwarden and son of the late vicar, went with another well known parishioner, Dunham Bird, to make an inventory for probate of Samuel's possessions. They noted the three beds, the six chairs and old table, the pewter on the dresser, the bundle of leather and

tools in the shop, and the animals in the yard. Altogether they considered them to be worth £18-5s-0d (NRO DN/INV 71/42).

Jane must have found life as a widow hard. She was still young – Samuel was only 35 years old at his death – and she did not grieve for long. When Simon Allen, a 'batchelor' from the village proposed, she accepted him eagerly and was married at Walcott by special licence the following May. No doubt some thought her too hasty, especially Samuel's brother John, and a quiet wedding in a neighbouring parish was expedient.

In August of the same year, 1711, a more prosperous villager, Thomas Smyth the miller, died. It was to him that Samuel Keeler and the others brought their sacks of corn to be ground, for all but the miserably poor, like Davy the thatcher, grew at least a little grain. Although the miller's house was rather larger than the cordwainer's, it was sparsely furnished. He had little more than two beds, a 'truckle' (trundle) bedstead, two 'coobbords', stools, chairs and an old table, but his kitchen was well-supplied with spits, hakes (pot hooks) and a churn, implying that he and his family lived moderately well. There were four cattle and six pigs in the yard, together with his horse. His real wealth lay in his windmill, valued at £30, and in the contents of the barn – wheat, barley, oats and hay – worth rather more. The sum total of his goods and chattels, as apprised by yet another Middleton, Robert, son of churchwarden William, was £89-3s-2d (NRO DN/INV 71/163).

Reverend James Farrer

The Reverend James Farrer owned a large house at Happisburgh and an equally imposing one, together with a very prosperous farm at Knapton. Although rector of Ridlington, it was to Knapton church that his wife Mary gave a large silver paten in 1703. At Knapton too, he had his study with books valued at £20 and a quantity of silver and linen. The farm stock included twenty bullocks, eight fat cattle and six horses. His Happisburgh house, which had at least ten rooms, was well furnished. There were a dozen chairs in the parlour alone and it was here that he kept his clock. In the kitchen, as well as the usual furniture and equipment, was a napkin press, a 'coal cradle' (his neighbours would have burnt driftwood) and a livery cupboard. The servants slept in the house, but their room contained only the bed. His possessions in both parishes, as estimated at his death in 1709, by Dunham Bird, were worth over £500 (NRO DN/INV 70/99).

A careful man, he stipulated that not more than £10 should be spent on his funeral. He was buried at his request in the chancel of Ridlington church, beneath a 'decent stone' with 'a very small inscription upon it'. The major part of his estate was left to his wife, passing at her death to John Fflight, her grandson by a previous marriage, providing the said John was 'very dutiful and obedient to his grandmother' and willing to be 'ruled and governed by her in all matters'. The Reverend James Farrer appears to have had doubts about the young man's character, for a further clause in his will demanded that John should not 'be out from his dwelling house late at nights … nor addict himself to noe gameing whether cards or dice or any other unlawful game whatsoever, but for a shilling a day and that not too often' (NRO NCC, will register, Famm, 142).

Jonathan Chaloner

Jonathan's uncle, the Revered Jonathan Chaloner, was vicar at Happisburgh from 1706 to 1727, and friend of the Reverend James Farrer. It was he who made provision for the poor of the parish to receive bread and clothing annually, and their children to be educated. His nephew, also Jonathan, held extensive property in Happisburgh, Lessingham, Suffield, Colby and Banningham which was inherited from his uncle. He lived for much of his life at Mundesley, but was buried beneath an imposing table-tomb in Happisburgh churchyard. The tomb carries his armorial bearings of adoring angels beneath the crest of a demi sea wolf.

Jonathan married three times: his first wife, Mary, and four of their children were buried nearby, as was Elizabeth, his third wife, who survived him. Beneath the inscription is the following line: 'N.B. Sarah his second wife was buried at Mundesley'.

No mention of Sarah's family was made in his will, although relatives of Mary and Elizabeth were remembered. To his widow he left 'the use of the little parlour and hall chamber' at Mundesley and 'such fruit, pulse or other garden stuff' as she needed. She was also left an annuity and £10 for mourning clothes – the same value as Edmund Sim's entire wardrobe.

Original Sources

While the making of a will might have been an activity restricted to the higher social classes, the widespread requirement for probate inventories to be compiled means that we are able to see detailed snapshots of the everyday lives of a broad spectrum of Happisburgh's residents. This chapter has given just a flavour of the rich tapestry of interconnected families who formed the core of Happisburgh's society for successive generations, while at the same time focussing on some of the tradesmen and labourers who also made a significant contribution to the village community. All of the original sources cited here, such as parish registers, wills and probate inventories, are held by the Norfolk Record Office, which also holds numerous other wills and probate inventories pertaining to Happisburgh's residents. All of these documents are free to be consulted by anyone wishing to find out more about the lives of parishioners past.

◇

Chapter 7

The Cruel Sea

Before the coming of the railway, when roads were in poor condition, much of the domestic traffic of the country was carried by little sailing ships – brigs, schooners, sloops and barges – travelling up and down the coast from the Thames to the Humber and Tyne. The Norfolk Coast has always been treacherous for seafarers, and the Haisbro Sand, about nine miles off Happisburgh, has been the cause of disaster for hundreds of vessels and claimed countless lives (Tikus 2003; 2004). Local author Ernest Suffling recalled 'I have known as many as seven steam vessels to be on them at the same time, not one of which ever floated again' (Suffling 1897, 172). Indeed, the sea off Happisburgh had

The divers sent by Trinity House to blow up the wrecks off Happisburgh in 1904.

become so littered with wrecked vessels that in 1904 Trinity House, fearing more disasters, sent a team of divers to blow them up!

A glance through the Happisburgh burial registers reveals a large number of entries pertaining to the unidentified bodies of sailors having been washed ashore and buried with due Christian ceremony in the churchyard. It is sobering to think of the many more ships which have been wrecked, and crew whose lives have been lost, which have gone unrecorded by history. This chapter tells the story of the more famous – perhaps infamous – wrecks which have occurred off the coast, and recounts the efforts by which Happisburgh's residents in days gone by attempted to reduce the dangers and save the lives of those unfortunately cast upon the sea. Among these efforts were the establishment of the Happisburgh beachmen, the foundation of the Happisburgh lifeboat and the erection of the Happisburgh lighthouses, all of which significantly improved the lot of sailors striving to navigate this difficult stretch of coast.

Rough seas have claimed the lives of many fishermen, but even the loss of a single boat could cause great hardship. In October 1800 a very high tide swept along the coast carrying two fishing boats out to sea. One was joint property of two poor men. Soon afterwards, the

Fishermen at work on Happisburgh beach in the 1930s. Their practices have remained largely unchanged for generations.

following report appeared in the newspaper: 'We have been told that application was made to a considerable farmer in the parish with an offer of payment for the use of his teams to draw the boats from the reach of the tide, which request was said to have been refused. We hope, however, that some urgent reason prevented the possibility of compliance as no other apology can atone for an act which appears to have driven two industrious families to the brink of ruin.' In a similar fashion, in the autumn of 1929 an unexpectedly high tide in the early morning swept away a boat and a large quantity of nets and gear. On this occasion a fund was organised in the village which helped considerably to cover the men's losses.

HMS Peggy

In the autumn of 1770 news reached England that the Spanish had occupied the Falkland Islands and expelled the small British force. With the possibility of war with Spain, ships were commissioned and press warrants sent to Newcastle to raise a large number of men for the Navy. The brig *Little Dick*, acting as a press tender, was ordered to Newcastle to take on board the newly conscripted men. However, so many had been raised that a number were embarked on *HMS Peggy*, an eight-gun 141-tonne naval sloop generally engaged in 'cruising against the smugglers' in the North Sea, and at that time moored at South Shields.

On Tuesday 18 December 1770, the *Peggy* under the command of Captain Richard Toby and the *Little Dick* set-sail in a fresh north-westerly gale, and by noon next day had anchored four miles off Cromer. The wind having changed to south-west by late afternoon, the two vessels continued along the Norfolk coast. But as darkness fell, and with a strengthening wind, Peggy lost her trysail mast. By 6pm it was raining hard and the pilot advised that they anchor. The *Little Dick* was signalled, but could no longer be seen. In the early hours of Thursday morning as Lieutenant George Robertson took over the morning watch on *Peggy*, the wind changed rapidly to the north-north-east, and amid squalls of driving snow, the ship was carried inshore. In an attempt to save the ship, orders were given to throw the casks of beer and water overboard, and as the sea rushed over her, the Captain commanded his men to cut away the mainmast and let the sheet anchor go, but it was too late. At 7am, with a sickening thud, *HMS Peggy* ground ashore on Happisburgh beach close to Town Gap. Waves beat over her, and it was not until noon when the tide had ebbed, that John Shepheard, bailiff of the manor of Happisburgh, together with a number of villagers, could bring wagons and horses along the beach.

Fifty-nine survivors were taken to safety and found shelter, but many, including the Captain, were completely exhausted. Lieutenant Robertson, a much younger and stronger man, assisted in the rescue and in bringing ashore the bodies of the dead. Among those who drowned were the master, purser, boatswain and surgeon. Thirty-two members of the Ship's Company lie buried in Happisburgh churchyard.

The *Little Dick* lost her foretopsail and staysail, but survived the storm, and with her Master, Joseph Holloway, praying 'for the assistance of God' she reached Great Yarmouth in safety. She was soon ordered to return to Happisburgh with two beach boats to take off the remnants of *HMS Peggy*'s crew. She reached her destination on 23 December and Captain Toby ordered his men to embark. Most did so, but fourteen of the press men, all seamen or shipwrights, stood firm. As the Captain reported: 'the new raised men who remained on the spot, appeared armed with clubs and refused to go on board the tender, on which myself and the Lieutenant used every means of inducing them to go on board, however ... they deserted.'

Unable to force them to obey, the Captain had

no option but to let them go. What rejoicing there must have been among the fourteen families when their men at length returned to Newcastle. The Lieutenant and the gunner remained to salvage as much of the stores as they could, and the wreck of the *HMS Peggy* was left half buried in the sand at high water mark for many years.

As is the rule after all naval wrecks, a Court Martial was held. It was concluded that the crew: 'did their utmost to preserve the said sloop and the loss was unavoidably occasioned by the badness of the weather.' Captain Toby had high praise for Lieutenant George Robertson: 'most of those who survived from the *Peggy* owe their preservation to that gentleman, who being blessed with uncommonly strong constitution retained his strength and senses when myself and most of the crew were deprived thereof, and he exerted himself in a most extraordinary manner.' The Lieutenant's reward was to be given command of the cutter *Prince George*.

One tangible link with *HMS Peggy* remains today. John Shepheard, the bailiff, procured one of her stern lanterns as a keepsake. It was passed on to his descendants, some of whom moved to Erpingham. For many years it hung in Abbots Hall near Aylsham until the last owner, Samuel Shepheard, died in 1974. It is now in the Maritime Museum, Great Yarmouth, where fitted with an electric light bulb, it illuminates a dark corridor.

HMS Invincible

Of the many sailing vessels wrecked off Happisburgh, *HMS Invincible* must have been by far the largest, and the loss of some 400 of the Ship's Company a great tragedy for so many families. On Monday 16 March 1801 the Invincible, a Third Rate 74-gun, sailed out of Great Yarmouth heavily laden with ordnance, ammunition, a great quantity of stores and almost 600 men. She had come from Chatham and put in to Yarmouth to collect orders before joining the Baltic Fleet under Admiral Sir Hyde Parker with Admiral Nelson as Second in Command, shortly before the battle of

Copenhagen. Rear Admiral of the Blue, Thomas Totty, was on board *Invincible*, his flag flying, with Captain John Rennie, 34 years of age and only very recently appointed to his first command.

Although the Master and the Pilot were thought to be well acquainted with the passage through Haisbro Gat, a strong tide and a fresh wind forced Invincible off course, and at about 2:30pm she struck Hammond's Knoll, a sandbank just east of Haisbro Sand. Some provisions were jettisoned to lighten the ship, and in late afternoon when she was labouring against a rising swell, the masts were cut away. It was hoped that she would float off at high water, which indeed she did, but having lost her rudder and with a heavy swell and freshening wind, she struck sand again. While the pumps were manned continuously in an effort to keep her above water, guns were fired at frequent intervals as a signal of distress.

Hope rose as the *Hunter*, a Revenue cutter on her way to Yarmouth, answered the distress signal, but to the dismay of *Invincible*'s crew, failed to send assistance. It was *The Nancy*, a smack fishing for cod, which came to the aid of the stricken ship. Her skipper, Daniel Grigson, anchored near by, and at midnight, when all hope of saving *Invincible* was gone, took aboard Admiral Totty and those of the crew who were little more than boys. *Invincible*'s own boats were lowered safely, but with the exception of the launch, were swept out to sea. The men were picked up later by a passing collier.

The *Nancy* stood by all night, hoping to rescue the remainder of the crew at daybreak, but to the horror of all on board, as the sky lightened, *Invincible* went down. All who could jumped on to the launch, which was soon overladen. Captain Rennie, the last to leave his ship, attempted to swim to the launch, but overcome with cold and exhaustion when almost within reach of the oars, lifted his hands to the sky, placed them over his face, and sank calmly beneath the waves. He was a brave and competent Officer, much respected by all under his command. Admiral Totty, writing his report the next day for the Court Martial, described the last

minutes of *Invincible* as follows: 'At daylight on Tuesday morning I observed that the Invincible had not a single Boat, either alongside or astern of her, and the Tide ran so strong that it was impossible to get the fishing Smack to her, but the moment the Tide slacked … she stretched under the *Invincible*'s Stern, endeavouring by all possible means to work up and get alongside of her; but before that could be accomplished the Ship went down in thirteen fathoms Water, and out of 600 persons that belonged to the *Invincible* there have not been above 190 saved and now living; several who were picked up by the launch died very soon afterwards. I am extremely grieved to inform you that Captain Rennie was among the number of those drowned; by his death the service has lost a truly zealous and intelligent Officer. … The horror of the scene … at the Moment the Ship went down far exceeds all power of description.'

Those who had reached the safety of *The Nancy* or the collier were landed at Great Yarmouth, where some were to die, no doubt from exposure in the cold North Sea. Soon after the Battle of Copenhagen (at which 256 men were lost, compared with about 400 from the *Invincible*) Nelson visited 'his men' lying injured in Yarmouth hospital.

During the days following the wreck, bodies were washed up on beaches along the coast. Cart load after cart load were brought to glebe land on the north side of Happisburgh Church, where a huge communal grave was dug. It was a gruesome task for the beachmen, and a horrifying sight for the villagers, who remembered it all their lives, and told of it to their grandchildren. In all, 119 bloated bodies were disposed of as quickly as possible. There is no record in the Parish Register of any burial service. Just seven years later, in 1808, the Burial of Drowned Persons Act decreed that all such should be given Christian burial in consecrated ground. Of all those who lost their lives on *Invincible*, the only recorded burial is of six men in Winterton churchyard.

As always after a wreck, many scoured the beach for anything of use which might be washed ashore. Among the flotsam from

Invincible was unexpected bounty. On 27 March, a large number of casks were seen floating at sea. Some 150 were brought ashore by a 'riding officer', found to contain brandy, and claimed for the Crown. But some casks escaped his notice, and were found washed up on the beach, to the great delight of some villagers. Unused to such luxury, they imbibed to excess, and one of them, Thomas Ansell, died the following day. He also was buried in Happisburgh churchyard.

At the Court Martial held in Sheerness Harbour on the last day of March, Admiral Totty expressed his 'entire approbation of the conduct of every Officer and Man for the strict order, regularity and subordination in every respect'. This was corroborated by all the surviving officers and several of the seamen who agreed that every exertion was made by the entire Ship's Company to save the vessel. The findings of the Court was that she was lost by running on shore through the ignorance of the two pilots (both of whom were drowned), and that the conduct of the Admiral, Captain, Officers and Ship's Company of His Majesty's late Ship the Invincible was 'highly meritorious'.

The resting place of the 119 men at Happisburgh was passed on by word of mouth, for no memorial stone marked the spot. This was cause of concern to Mrs Mary Cator who was living in Happisburgh during the first part of the 20th century. After consultation with the then vicar, the Reverend Aldous Hitchcock, she wrote to the *Eastern Daily Press* in August 1913 suggesting that a subscription be raised for a memorial to 'so many of Nelson's gallant men'. At first the Editor welcomed the idea, proposed that a committee be formed to oversee the project, and offered Mrs Cator 'the best thanks of the county'. Sir Samuel Hoare of Sidestrand Hall gave his enthusiastic support, and donations flowed in. However, not everyone agreed. An anonymous correspondent writing under the name of 'Steam Drifter' harangued Mrs Cator for having insufficient evidence of the burials, and considered it ridiculous and absurd that a memorial be erected. Other letters were published from 'Dulce et Decorum est Pro Patria

Mori' who felt it would 'be better to devote our energies to the living'. Could these two correspondents have been somewhat piqued at not being invited to join Mrs Cator's committee? The Reverend Aldous Hitchcock certainly thought so.

By early October Mrs Cator had received nearly £100 – almost enough to erect a plain granite cross – which she now suggested be a memorial to all seamen known to be buried at Happisburgh, and also to 'those who perished from the Invincible off the Norfolk coast'. Sir Samuel Hoare offered to double his subscription, but the Editor of the *Eastern Daily Press* was growing uneasy. In his leader of 6 October 1913, he advised that the whole project be dropped. 'Perhaps at some future time it might be revived on a more sure basis.' If purchased, the memorial would probably have the reputation 'of being a monument to the wrong people in the wrong place' .

Mrs Cator had little option but to return the money. But she was tenacious, and did not give up easily. When the bells of St Mary's church were rehung in 1924, she gave a treble bell and had it inscribed 'In memory of Nelson's men wrecked off Haisbro in 1801'. Those who perished from HMS Invincible have never been forgotten.

In time, the glebe land where donkeys had once grazed, was incorporated into the churchyard, and the lower portion used for burials. But the mound on top of the hill remained untouched – until, that is, a drainage trench was dug in 1988 to take rain water from the church roof. Then, no more than three feet deep, skeletons were found, evidently buried in haste and in disorder. The remains were reburied and prayers said, perhaps the first time that those young men had been given a Christian burial. There was now little room for doubt. Ten years later, thanks to the suggestion of Peter Rope, a retired naval officer, the present *HMS Invincible* was contacted. The Captain and Ship's Company responded with much interest, and joined with St Mary's Parochial Church Council in providing a simple memorial stone.

The memorial to the crew of HMS Invincible *which was erected in the churchyard in July 1998.*

On Tuesday 24 July 1998 St Mary's church was filled to overflowing. Many had come from far afield: members of the Nelson Society, ex-Wrens, a descendant of Captain John Rennie, and, as was so very appropriate, the Second in Command, the Chaplain and eight members of the Ship's Company of the present *HMS Invincible*. In his address the Rector, the Reverend Dr Richard Hines spoke of our 'gratitude and admiration ... for the dignified example and perseverance of (the Ships Company of *Invincible*) as together they faced death in the course of doing their duty'. The Memorial in the churchyard could be 'interpreted as a gesture of Christian faith ... that even in their most desperate moments those who perished out in that cold North Sea ... did not perish beyond the love and presence of Almighty God'.

In bright sunshine and with a fresh wind, the congregation gathered on the mound, and within sight of Hammond's Knoll the prayers of dedication were said.

The memorial stone bears the inscription:

On 16 March 1801, HMS INVINCIBLE
was wrecked off Happisburgh when
on her way to join a fleet with
Admiral Nelson at Copenhagen.
The day following, the Ship sank with
the loss of some four hundred lives.
One hundred and nineteen members
of the Ship's Company lie buried here.
"And the sea gave up the dead
That were in it ..."
Revelation 20:13
This memorial stone was given jointly
by the Parochial Church Council and
the Officers and Ship's Company of
HMS Invincible, 1998

A thrill passed through the gathered company as a bugler from *Invincible* sounded the 'Last Post' – and after a silence broken only by the freshening wind, the 'Reveille'. The men of HM's Late Ship *Invincible* had at last received a fitting tribute to their memory.

Hunter

Having failed to send assistance during the wrecking of *HMS Invincible*, on 18 February 1807 the Yarmouth revenue cutter *Hunter* was herself caught in a storm which dashed her on to Haisbro Sands. She was then driven towards the shore and beached to the north of Cart Gap, with the loss of all hands – more than 40 men.

HMS Ranger

HMS Ranger, another Yarmouth-based Revenue cutter and *Hunter*'s replacement, patrolled much of the east coast and was greatly dreaded by smugglers. On the evening of 13 October 1822, Captain John Sayers ordered two small boats, each with a crew of seven, to put out and search inshore waters. While Ranger stood by, the wind increased and soon a furious gale was blowing. The crew could not hold her and she was swept onto a sandbank close to shore. Allegations were made that Happisburgh folk lining the clifftop paid no heed to the distress signals and cries for help from the desperate crew. These charges were denied, but it may well have been that certain villagers saw no reason why they should help their enemies who hindered their unlawful occupation. Next morning the wreck of *HMS Ranger* was swept to the shore close to the spot where the remains of the *Hunter* lay.

Young England

In October 1876, the barque *Young England* was wrecked off the coast of Happisburgh. In the midst of the maelstrom, thirteen members of the crew managed to launch the ship's long-boat and headed for the shore, but before they could reach it they were carried before the wind some twelve miles south to the shores of Winterton. Unsure of where best to land, they paused to consider their next course of action, but their indecision proved to be fatal, as the sea overwhelmed their vessel and cast the crew into the water. Only one small boy survived, washed up on Winterton beach with a broken leg, the rest perished. The captain of the *Young England*, his wife and ten of the crew who had remained with the vessel were all rescued by a tug from Yarmouth. In a cruel twist of fate, two days after the wreck, the bodies of six of the crew were washed ashore at Happisburgh – the very place they were heading for in their ill-fated longship. The men, whose number included the ship's 6'4" Norwegian mate, were buried together in a grave at the eastern end of the church, their resting place marked by a gravestone depicting an expertly crafted anchor carved by one Barnabas Barrett of Norwich (Suffling 1897, 173–4).

The grave of the six seamen of the Young England, whose bodies were washed ashore at Happisburgh in 1876.

The Beachmen

Almost every seaside village between Cromer and Lowestoft had a company of beachmen. These companies made it their business to go to the aid of any ship in distress, and whatever the weather or risks involved, the flare of rockets and boom of minute guns from a stricken vessel never went unheeded. There was great competition between companies, for the first men aboard could claim right of salvage. On reaching the vessel, and before rescue began, terms of employment were settled, and the beachmen drove a hard bargain. But their work was arduous and fraught with danger, and on many occasions they earned nothing at all.

By the middle of the 19th century, Happisburgh fishermen had formed a company and by the 1870s had acquired a fast sailing yawl, *Friendship*, built at a cost of £160. Some money was subscribed, but each of the 28 men who had part ownership contributed £5-10s, despite the fact that their average weekly wage was about 12s. A crew of 13 manned her and dragging the yawl 200 yards over loose sand at low tide and launching her through the breakers was no easy task. Hauling her ashore and up the Gap was even harder, and often took a full two hours. The Royal National Lifeboat Institution established a station here in 1866, but the lifeboat, also manned by beachmen, was one of the smaller class usually working inshore, so it was the *Friendship* who generally went to the assistance of vessels stranded on the Haisbro Sands.

The beachmen also collected all salvageable goods washed ashore. Their headquarters and storehouse was a shed on the cliff top beside the old lifeboat house. For many years a large and colourful ship's figurehead washed up from a

This photograph from the early 20th century shows a typical collection of flotsam and jetsam collected from the beach by the villagers.

The beachmen's headquarters and storehouse was a shed on the cliff top beside the old lifeboat house.

wreck stood by the doorway. The collection and use of such material was a long tradition, as had been noted by Daniel Defoe, who when riding from Great Yarmouth to Cromer in 1724 who surprised to see that 'all the way from Winterton, the farmers and country people had scarce a barn or a shed, or a stable, nay, not the pales of their yards and gardens, not a hogstye, not a necessary-house, but what was built of old planks, beams, wales and timbers, etc., the wrecks of ships and ruins of mariners' and merchants' fortunes, and some places were whole yards filled and piled up very high with the same stuff laid up, as I supposed to sell for the like building purposes, as there should be occasion' (Defoe 1949, 97).

The Coastguard

The first Happisburgh Coastguard station was established in 1820, with dwellings to house an officer and five men. At the time, they were known as the Preventative Service. Coastal erosion threatened the cottages, and in 1879 new premises were built further inland. The staff was reduced to four, and later to two. In 1957, another Coastguard station was built on adjoining land, but in 1979 the regular Coastguards were withdrawn.

Ben Dobson was one of the Happisburgh Coastguards from 1940 until his death in 1955. He was involved in rescuing the crew of the Admiralty trawler *HMS Dungeness*, which was bombed off Happisburgh and run aground in November 1940 (NHER 34156; Tikus 2003, 23), and also played an active part in the aftermath of the 1953 floods. In 1956, he was awarded a posthumous Bronze medal for bravery from the French government for his role in rescuing the crew of the French trawler *St Pierre Eglise* when she ran aground at Waxham in February 1955.

A second long-serving member of the Coastguard, Don Cox, was awarded the Queen's Commendation for brave conduct for the part he played when an aircraft from RAF Watton caught fire and crashed off Happisburgh in December 1956. Mr Cox rushed straight to the beach, where he saw two men standing in the water on an offshore sandbar. He waded out to

Ben Dobson

Don Cox

them, and finding one man injured, aided the other in fighting against the current and swell to escort both men back to the shore. When asked about his achievement, Mr Cox reportedly stated 'It was all in the day's work.'

The Rocket Brigade

In the early 19th century, Captain George Manby, artilleryman and barrack master at Great Yarmouth, devised a system of getting a line to a stranded ship by means of a small mortar, and used it himself in 1808. Later he developed a method of hauling shipwrecked men ashore in a cradle or breeches buoy. The mortar was superseded by a rocket with a range of about 100 yards (Storey 2009, 116–17). Life saving apparatus of this kind was installed at Happisburgh in 1859. It was taken to the scene of a wreck on a wagon, and was either manhandled or pulled by farm horses. For practice purposes a rocket pole was erected on the cliff top to represent the mast of a vessel. The Rocket Brigade trained regularly and Life Saving Apparatus competitions were held at Winterton, which the Happisburgh team often won.

The Rocket Brigade was disbanded in the early 1980s. Navigational aids have much improved, and as shipping is of greater tonnage, most vessels now keep on the far side of Haisbro Sand, but during the years that the Rocket Brigade was stationed at Happisburgh, twenty-two lives were saved.

During a violent gale and snow storm in 1916 the schooner *Angela* of London was driven ashore near Cart Gap. Burning flares alerted the crew of the lifeboat and the rocket brigade, but as it was impossible to launch the lifeboat in the extremely difficult conditions the life-saving apparatus was used. A line was fired on board and, after much effort, five exhausted men were brought to safety by breeches buoy.

On 30 January 1940, a report reached the Air Raid Warden's Post at 3:30am that a vessel was on fire about one mile off shore due to enemy action. A further message reported that the ship had beached at Walcott Gap. Snow had been falling all night and had been drifting. The Life Saving Apparatus was loaded on a trailer by members of the Rocket Brigade who tried to make the journey by road. The snow was too deep, and only with great difficulty were they able to return and carry the equipment 1½ miles along the beach. It was still dark when they reached Walcott Gap and found the *Tautmillar*, a vessel of about 3,700 tons. They made the deck by rope ladder, and found that the fire in the

B.E. Trett of the Rocket Brigade guarding the wreck of the Tautmillar *in 1940.*

The Rocket Brigade's practice pole on the clifftops, with the collapsing ruins of the original coastguard houses in the background to the left, and the beachmen's hut and the lifeboathouse to the right.

Members of the Rocket Brigade practise establishing rescue lines under the watchful eye of the Coastguard.

hold was dying down. One man, Bruno Adler, a Latvian unable to speak English and in a very exhausted condition, was found on board wearing all of his clothes and with towels wrapped around his head. Later, it was discovered that he had been knocked unconscious and when the Captain ordered all to abandon ship, he was left for dead, reviving to find himself alone. Seven crew were killed and twelve had taken to the small boats. A watch was kept on the *Tautmillar* for three weeks by Rocket Brigade members until she was towed to Yarmouth for repairs; sadly, the following year she was sunk by enemy action.

The hardest work was pulling the lifeboat back up to the lifeboat house, and for this two more horses were used, making ten in all.

The Happisburgh Lifeboats

'The Norfolk Association for Saving the Lives of Ship-wrecked Mariners' was formed in November 1823 and set about establishing lifeboat stations along the coast. In 1858 these stations were taken over by the Royal National Life boat Institution, who established the first lifeboat station on the cliffs at Happisburgh in 1866 at a cost of £189.

In August 1866, the first lifeboat, the *Huddersfield*, arrived in Happisburgh. She was a 32-foot self-righting type pulling ten oars, built by Woolfe of Shadwell at a cost of £240. She had been paid for by the people of Huddersfield, who had raised £1000 towards the cost of the boat and its maintenance, and the boat was given free conveyance on the railway to Stalham.

Happisburgh's first lifeboat station, established in 1866.

Launching the lifeboat: two horses pulled the boat-carriage down the Gap while the crew and onlookers hauled on ropes behind to act as a break. (From the Neil Storey Archive)

Once on the beach, six more horses were hooked on, with a single horse leading, to take the boat into the sea.

The August bank holiday practice launch often attracted a considerable crowd of visitors, as can be seen in this pair of photographs from the early 20th century.

The Happisburgh lifeboat crew, c.1920. Back row: Tom Lawson, 'Shirhy' Hannant, 'Titler' Sadd, Cannon Harvey (Cox), Ted Jones, John Siely, Billy Hannant, 'Polar' Mason. Front row: (?)Benny Wiseman, George 'Doddy' Grimmer, (?)Jimmy Wiseman, unknown, unknown.

The lifeboat crew was called out by a runner shouting, 'Ship ahoy!' This cry summoned horses from neighbouring farms as well as men, for their help was needed to launch the boat. Two horses pulled the boat-carriage down the Gap while the crew and onlookers hauled on ropes behind to act as a break. Six more horses were hooked on, with a single horse leading, to take the boat into the sea. To avoid sending the animals into very deep water, they were shackled on to the back wheels of the carriage. The hardest work was pulling the boat back up to the lifeboat house, and for this two more horses were used, making ten in all, although only eight horses were generally used at a practice. Such practice launches were carried out four times a year and the August bank holiday launch often attracted a considerable crowd of visitors as well as local people, and was an important event in village life. For the first 23 years of its service, the horses which pulled the lifeboat were supplied by Mr William Wilkins, whose wife received a gratuity of £5 from the RNLI on his death in 1890.

After long service, near disaster struck on 23 January 1884 when the *Huddersfield* went to the aid of the schooner *Edith* of Padstow, wrecked just offshore, for as *Huddersfield* approached the vessel she was swept across its deck. The shore party manned a rope and succeeded in pulling her off, but she then overturned, throwing out the crew. Two men swam to the shore and, fortunately, the remaining eleven managed to regain the boat.

The original Huddersfield was withdrawn in 1887, having saved 51 lives in its 40 years of service. The 34-foot *Huddersfield 2* was brought in to replace it, the boat again being provided by the townspeople of Huddersfield. A third and final lifeboat, the *Jacob And Rachel Vallentine*, was sent to Happisburgh in 1907. She was named as desired by the donor, Mr Samuel Vallentine, a prominent member of the Jewish community in Brixton. In his will he requested that a lifeboat be stationed on the east coast within one year of his death. The inauguration of the *Jacob and Rachel* was presided over by Mrs Cator, who gave the crew a dinner. Mr Tijou and Colonel

Birkbeck spoke and Mrs Tijou broke a bottle of champagne over the lifeboat.

In 1926 the RNLI decided to close the Happisburgh station, as it was thought that the motor lifeboat at Cromer could cover this area adequately. The *Jacob and Rachel* was moved to Sea Palling, and thence to Whitby where she remained in service until at least 1947. During her service at Happisburgh she had launched sixteen times and saved nineteen lives. There were four Coxswains during the 60 years of the all-weather lifeboats at Happisburgh, one of whom, John Cannon, had been awarded a Silver Medal on his retirement for his long and valuable service in 1886. The old lifeboat station was left to fall into ruin, and was eventually demolished in the 1950s.

In 1965, the RNLI established an Inshore Lifeboat (ILB) station at Happisburgh, in a new lifeboat house adjacent to the Beach Road car park. This was one of the first 'D class' inflatable lifeboats and was placed on service in June, having been paid for by members of the of Norwich Round Table. Inshore boats can be launched with the minimum of delay, can do well over 20 knots and can keep up this speed for at least two hours; their normal crew is two

and they can carry up to ten people. The lifeboat was in service each summer, from April to October, going to the aid of everything from trawlers, fishing boats, swimmers and, as time went on, windsurfers, divers, jet-skiers and kiteboarders. On 13 September 1994 a new 'D class' ILB was placed on service, named the *Colin Martin* in memory of a local man who lost his life in a tragic accident.

In December 2002 the lifeboat launching ramp was washed away overnight due to massive erosion. The RNLI, working closely with North Norfolk District Council, was able to open a fully operational station at Cart Gap within three months and the boat remained in service throughout the change over. The original station is now used for training and souvenir sales. Following this move, in October 2003 the latest 'D Class' lifeboat arrived at Happisburgh, the *Spirit of Berkhamsted*. The naming ceremony was held in Berkhamsted, as that RNLI branch had raised the funds for this boat and won awards for doing so in such a short time.

April 2009 saw the Happisburgh lifeboat move forward again, with a two-year trial of an 'Atlantic 75 B Class' lifeboat, *Friendly Forester II*, working alongside the existing 'D Class' boat.

The dedication ceremony for the new Happisburgh lifeboat in 1965, presided over by the Reverend Large.

The Friendly Forester II *came to Happisburgh for a two-year trial in 2009. This trial was so successful that its stationing was made permanent in 2011.*

The successful operation of the Happisburgh lifeboat requires a large group of volunteers. This photograph shows the team in December 2010. Front row (l–r): Sharlotte Siely, Jake Munday, Colin Fleming, Dawn Phenix, Cedric Cox, Cubitt Siely, Matt Bales, Tony Phenix, Tony Godfree, Ross Scannell and Steve Kinsey. Back row (l–r): Alex Willoughby, Arron Coe, Bob Man, Pete James, Eddie Randall, Les Bennet, Andy Goldsmith, Mark Defraine, Justin Arnold, Lee Wilkins, Christian Larter, Alex Williams and Robert Ferguson.

This acquisition necessitated the building of a new ramp to improve access to the beach for the larger boat, and a new lifeboat station was required to house the two lifeboats together with new training and crew facilities. The boat came from the reserve fleet, is approximately 15 years old and started service as the station boat in Poole, Dorset. This trial period was so successful, that in January 2011 the *Friendly Forester II* was made permanent.

The Happisburgh lifeboats have been involved in numerous rescues since 1965, but one of the largest, involving working with many other lifeboats, helicopters and other agencies was on 11 November 1996, when the tug *Beaver 2* capsized. One crewman was recovered and

In October 1989, the trawler De Vrouw Melanie *drifted onto a sand bar and was carried to the shore at high tide, becoming stuck fast on the beach at Cart Gap. Electricians boarded her to carry out repairs, and after several attempts she and her six -man crew were refloated with the aid of a tug.*

transferred ashore to a waiting ambulance, but there was unfortunately the loss of one life. Another serious incident occurred on 18 August 2007, when nine divers were overdue 3.5 miles off Happisburgh. Cromer and Sheringham lifeboats, as well as a Helicopter were also called upon and Happisburgh lifeboat found the nine divers, returning seven ashore with Sheringham lifeboat landing the other two.

Although best known for his atmospheric use of colour in scenes of storm and sunset, J.M.W. Turner also painted a great number of miniatures to be engraved as vignettes for use as book illustrations. In the late 1820s, he painted several scenes from along the East Anglian coast, including this view of 'Hasborough Sands'. The painting is in pencil, watercolour and bodycolour on grey–blue paper and measures 21cm x 17cm. The original sold at auction in 2003 for £65,725. (© Christie's Images/ The Bridgeman Art Library)

Chapter 8

◇

Happisburgh's Lighthouses

by Patrick Tubby

(Chairman, Happisburgh Lighthouse Trust)

To the people of Norfolk, Happisburgh Lighthouse, with its distinctive coloured bands, must be one of the county's most instantly recognisable buildings. This wasn't always the case – for almost 200 years the lighthouse had existed in quiet solitude – but all that changed in the late 1980s when Trinity House, the general lighthouse authority for England and Wales, announced their intention to discontinue the use of the light. Over the last two decades successive lighthouse trustees and volunteers have sought

to attract publicity and keep the image of the lighthouse firmly in the minds of the general populace.

The need for a lighthouse at Happisburgh was highlighted in October 1789, when a severe storm saw the loss of over 60 ships and around 600 lives off the Norfolk coast. At the time primitive coal beacons existed at Cromer, Winterton and Caister, but there was nothing in the Happisburgh area and proposals for two new lighthouses at Happisburgh were swiftly drawn up.

An aerial photograph of the lighthouse taken in June 1985. In the background are the houses at the end of Beach Road which were lost to the sea in the 1990s. (© Norfolk County Council; Photograph by D.A. Edwards: TG3830/H/AYN12)

A architectural cross-section through the Happisburgh High Light, from the Trinity House archives. (© Trinity House, used with permission)

In 1790, construction began on two towers to form a leading line clear of the southern end of the notorious Haisbro Sands. The lighthouses were set about four hundred yards apart; the High Light, set on a hill inland was eighty five feet tall, and the cliff top low light twenty feet shorter.

An early architectural elevation drawing of the Happisburgh High Light, from the Trinity House archives. (© Trinity House, used with permission)

On 1 January 1791 the lighthouses came into operation. Each tower was surmounted by a lantern holding a number of Argand oil lamps placed in front of polished reflectors – these were fixed lights (i.e. not flashing). Keeping the lights in line one above the other enabled ships to enter the sheltered stretch of water between the Sands and the shore known as The Would. Other local improvements at the time saw the Newarp lightship established on the Newarp bank seventeen miles south-east of Happisburgh in 1790; the conversion to oil lights of both Winterton and Cromer lighthouses in 1791

and 1792 respectively; and the discontinuing of the sometimes confusing lights at Caister.

Little is known of the Happisburgh lighthouses' early history, which would suggest that no major incidents took place, although as was described in the previous chapter on 16 March 1801 *HMS Invincible* was wrecked on the Hammond Knoll, a sandbank about fifteen miles east of Happisburgh. In the years since the lighthouse has been established this is by far the worst maritime disaster to take place in the vicinity of Happisburgh. The *Invincible* however, did not founder for want of a more powerful navigational light, for she grounded on the Knoll in the early afternoon whilst attempting to navigate Haisborough Gat. Strong winds and a heavy tide had conspired to push the vessel several miles off course which resulted in her loss with over four hundred of the ship's company.

In 1832 the Haisbro lightship was established to mark the northern end of the Haisbro Sands twelve miles north of Happisburgh village. Two fixed white lights were shown at an elevation of 36 feet above sea level with a range of ten miles.

Haisbro Lightship seen here on station in 1936. This vessel was one of several built for Trinity House by R. Stephenson & Co., Hebburn, between 1888 and 1892.

We know that each of the Happisburgh lighthouses was attended by two full time keepers, and from the first national census records of 1841, the keepers at the High Light were Edward Garwood and John Knowles, whilst the Low Light was attended by James Thatcher with his son Charles as assistant.

Improvements were made to both towers in 1868. Prismatic glass optics from the Birmingham factory of Chance Brothers were installed.

THE LIGHTHOUSE, HAPPISBURGH.

This postcard of the lighthouse in 1902 clearly shows the two gas holders which were installed to store the gas generated on the site. The postmark is 1907 and the message, from Agnes Gentry to George Danes, says 'Do you recognise the photo? It was taken when we had the gas here – the black building at the end is the Gas House. That's ME standing at the gate 5 years ago.'

These replaced the reflectors and oil lamp systems, now just one oil lamp would be placed in the centre of each optic, rather than an oil lamp in front of each reflector. To house the optics the wooden lanterns on each tower were replaced with larger helically framed lanterns made of cast iron. These lanterns had diagonal framing so that the lights were visible from all points to seaward. The optics gave the High Light an improved range of 17 miles, and the Low Light a range of 15 miles.

Happisburgh became a pioneering lighthouse in 1872 with the introduction of gas lighting on an experimental basis. As the lighthouse was not sufficiently close to any mains gas supply, the gas was manufactured within the grounds of the High Light. Coal was brought to Happisburgh by sea, and at the High Light was heated to create a fuel known as coal gas or cannel gas. The gas was stored in two gas holders alongside the lighthouse. The system was devised by John Wigram, who wanted to compare his new gas system with the oil lamps still in use at the Low Light. Although the gas system readily appeared superior to the oil

lamps, Trinity House were reluctant to convert other lights to gas.

Although not largely adopted elsewhere, the gas system continued in use at Happisburgh for over thirty years. Interestingly, in the 1891 census the second Assistant Lighthouse Keeper was 38-year old John Phillips Avery, who ten years later was listed as 'gas maker'. Following the installation of a paraffin vapour burner as the main light in 1904, the staffing at the lighthouse was reduced to two keepers, and from the 1911 census we know that Avery was still in service at Happisburgh as Assistant Keeper.

Over the last 20 years, the erosion at Happisburgh has regularly kept the village in the spotlight. Sadly though, this isn't a new problem – in the early 1880s the cliff top Low Light was becoming threatened by cliff erosion. Improvements were also being made in lighting technology and having two lighthouses at Happisburgh to maintain and staff was expensive. Thus Trinity House took the decision to discontinue the Low Light and install an occulting light in the remaining tower (i.e. the period the light displayed is greater than the time it is eclipsed). At Happisburgh this was achieved by a clockwork mechanism which lowered a metal hood to eclipse the light source for five seconds every half minute. It was also at this time that the lighthouse was first painted in its now familiar red and white bands. The Sands themselves were now also marked by a third lightship, the Would, established in 1880.

Stripped of salvageable equipment the Low Light was sold by tender to the highest bidder and demolished in 1886. Local author Ernest Suffling described the demolition process in some detail: 'First, a line of bricks was taken out all round, about 14 ft to 16 ft from the ground. Into this gap the heads of a number of strong props, or rough battens, were placed, the other ends being firmly planted in the ground. Men then dug away the foundation of the tower, as much as they considered prudent, so as to leave it in a very weak state. A load of faggots was then placed beneath the supporting logs, and lighted. Soon the logs began to burnt through and fall away one by one; and then, without a moment's warning, the whole fabric, 80 ft in height, came to the ground with a dull roar, amid a chaos of smoke, dust and flames. When the clouds of smoke had blown away, it was discovered that the watch-room had come down intact, without even breaking the floor or glass windows, and this from a height, from ground-line to floor of the watch-room, of 60 ft!' (Suffling 1897, 177).

Very few contemporary images of the Low Light survive. There is a sketch showing both lighthouses by Miss A. Turner in Dawson Turner's illustrated edition of Blomefield's *History of Norfolk*, currently in the British Library. During the writing of this book, a local resident drew the authors' attention to small drawings of the High Light and the Low Light which appeared on the corner of an admiralty chart produced in the 1880s and which noted the decommissioning date for the Low Light. Although we have not been able to locate an original copy of this map yet, a photograph of the Low Light illustration is included here.

The 1868 Chance optic was eventually reused when Southwold lighthouse was established in

The Low Light, as depicted on an admiralty chart from the late 1880s. We are grateful to John Marshall for drawing this to our attention.

1890. This little part of Happisburgh's old Low Light has continued to be used to provide the main light at Southwold for over 120 years. A new improved system is being installed in Southwold in 2011, but the old Happisburgh optic will still be used to provide the emergency light should the main systems fail.

The paraffin light installed in 1904, although producing a very bright incandescent light, was quite labour intensive, and following the end of the First World War, Trinity House began to look ways of reducing their costs at some of their less significant lights. Acetylene-powered lights began to be adopted at certain lighthouses, and in 1929 Happisburgh became the fifth manned lighthouse to be converted to acetylene. This made it possible to dispense with the need for resident keepers, though a local attendant was employed to check the light periodically. The two adjoining keepers' cottages were subsequently sold and became private dwellings.

Happisburgh Lighthouse was converted to run on mains electricity in 1947, with a diesel generator as back-up. The acetylene system was retained as an emergency light and would automatically come in to operation should the mains and generator fail. During these improvements the character of the light was altered to a light flashing three times in six seconds followed by a 24 second eclipse (as it still does today).

During the late 1950s, over 70 years after being demolished, the foundations of the old Low Light were exposed by the erosion of the cliffs and finally fell on to the beach. Several photographs survive of the eroding ruins of the Low Light, including an image taken by Jo Sharplin, who holidayed in Happisburgh with her parents during July 1956 and who used her pre-War Zeiss–Ikon camera to photograph the ruins. We are very fortunate that Ms Sharplin still has the negatives, and has kindly allowed them to be scanned to illustrate this book. The erection of the sea defences in the late 1950s slowed the rate of the erosion, so that the remains of the Low Light remained largely unchanged until the late 1980s, when breaches in the defences caused the erosion to accelerate again. When walking along the beach towards Cart Gap today, it is still possible to see a few remnants of sea-smoothed red brickwork at the low water line.

Following the removal of the resident light keepers at the end of the 1920s, Happisburgh

The remains of the Low Light can only now be seen clearly during very low tides, as was the case in March 2011.

This photograph, taken by Jo Sharplin on 28 July 1956, clearly shows the brick foundations of the Low Light eroding from the cliff.

Lighthouse operated almost anonymously for the next half a century. All that changed in the mid-1980s when the 1987 Navigational Aid Review was announced. These reviews are generally carried out around every five years to assess the number and mix of navigational aids and their current operational and economic worth. The 1987 Review was one of the most severe; it proposed to discontinue five lighthouses, four lightships, several fog signals, and numerous buoys and minor lights. Both Happisburgh lighthouse and the offshore Haisbro lightship were on the list of doomed lights – though the lightship, which was expensive to maintain, was to be replaced by a modern navigation buoy with a reduced range.

A more recent incarnation of the Haisbro Lightship, shown on station in the 1970s. This ship was built by Philip & Son Ltd, Dartmouth, in 1963. (© Trinity House, used with permission)

It seemed originally that the news of the loss of the lighthouse was not really picked up until an actual closure date of 13 June was announced in early 1988. Kay Swann, a local marine geophysicist, spearheaded a campaign aimed at persuading Trinity House to retain Happisburgh as a working lighthouse. Miss Swann began canvassing opinion from local marine users, especially among the local fishing communities between Wells and Great Yarmouth.

Trinity House initially gave the lighthouse a two month 'stay of execution' to look again at their decision to discontinue the light and also to allow locals to put their case together. Trinity House came back adamant that the lighthouse was surplus to requirements; but the people of Happisburgh would not be thwarted – there was concern that even with an increased range

on Cromer lighthouse there was still an area of sea close inshore where no light would be visible if Happisburgh was to be turned off. Kay Swann and her team went back to Trinity House and asked if it would be possible for a local Trust to be set up to take over the running of the lighthouse. This, in theory, was feasible. However, Trinity House could only dispose of a working lighthouse to an established lighthouse authority (this would be similar to a local harbour authority, and not surprisingly, Happisburgh was beyond the jurisdiction of Great Yarmouth, the nearest authority). For Happisburgh to be operated independently, the Friends of Happisburgh Lighthouse, the initial campaign group, would have to establish themselves as a local lighthouse authority, which would require a Private Members Bill and an Act of Parliament. A fund-raising campaign to meet the costs of the Parliamentary matters began and was helped enormously by a donation of £15,000 from the National Westminster Bank.

After a seventeen month passage through Parliament, the Happisburgh Lighthouse Bill

Happisburgh Lighthouse Act 1990

CHAPTER xvi

ARRANGEMENT OF SECTIONS

Section
1. Short title.
2. Interpretation.
3. Establishment and constitution of Trust.
4. Trust to be local lighthouse authority.
5. Powers of Trust to manage lighthouse undertaking, etc.
6. Dissolution of association.
7. Winding up of affairs of Trust.
8. Saving for Trinity House.
9. Costs of Act.

SCHEDULE—Constitution of Happisburgh Lighthouse Trust.

The cover of the Lighthouse Act, which gained Royal Assent on 25 April 1990.

Her Majesty Queen Elizabeth the Queen Mother visited Happisburgh lighthouse and the church in July 1990.

Television presenter Anneka Rice addresses the assembled crowd with a loudhailer during the filming of the BBC programme Challenge Anneka in August 1990.

received Royal Assent on 25 April 1990. The Happisburgh Lighthouse Trust was formed as a local lighthouse authority to operate and maintain the light. Trustees were initially drawn from parish and district councillors and a representative of the local fishermen's association.

Happisburgh Lighthouse Trust took control of the lighthouse on 1 August 1990, an occasion that was marked a few days earlier with a visit from Her Majesty Queen Elizabeth the Queen Mother. While in Happisburgh, the Queen Mother also took the opportunity to visit the parish church, as she has family ties to the village: the deeds for St Mary's show that her brother, Michael Bowes Lyon, owned it for a while – he married Elizabeth Margaret Cator in February 1928.

In late August 1990, at the end of the Trust's first month in charge, the lighthouse was the subject of an episode of the BBC television programme *Challenge Anneka* with Anneka Rice. In just 36 hours, the lighthouse was completely repainted, inside and out, as well as having the stand-by light replaced with a battery back-up, and the lighthouse drive completely relaid. In 1997 it was wrongly reported that the *Challenge Anneka* paintwork had been badly applied and flaked off requiring the repainting of the lighthouse, a mistaken story which was unfortunately taken up by the national press. In reality,

although the paint had faded, it was an interim coat of paint applied in 1994 which had flaked so badly. Sadly, the national media failed to set the record straight, and it is hoped that this book might go some way to redress the balance.

Over the last twenty years the lighthouse has attracted various publicity, open days were reintroduced for the first time in over 60 years in 1991 and, in an effort to supplement the income of the Trust, it has been used as a film and television location. Music videos, commercials, and television dramas have all been filmed at the lighthouse, including an episode of the ITV drama *Kingdom* starring Stephen Fry and the music video for the Ellie Goulding single 'The Writer' from her debut album *Lights*.

Happisburgh lighthouse is still owned by Trinity House, but the Happisburgh Lighthouse Trust is responsible for the maintenance and operation of the lighthouse. The original Friends group set up to campaign for the retention of the lighthouse has now evolved into a separate fundraising charity to augment the work done by the Trustees. Happisburgh lighthouse is the only independently operated lighthouse in the United Kingdom, and is inspected by the Inspector of Seamarks on an annual basis.

In 2009, the Friends were delighted to announce that Her Royal Highness The Princess Royal had accepted an invitation to become

Chairman of the Happisburgh Lighthouse Trust, Patrick Tubby, demonstrates the extent of the offshore Haisbro Sands to HRH The Princess Royal during her visit to the lighthouse in May 2010.

Patron of the Friends of Happisburgh Light-house and in this capacity she visited the light-house on 12 May 2010 to mark the 20th anniversary of control passing to the independent Happisburgh Lighthouse Trust.

The role of lighthouses in general has changed greatly over the last 220 years. When Happisburgh was established there were very few lights around our coasts, and most homes would have been lit by candles or primitive oil lamps; nowadays lighthouses have to be visible against a backdrop of bright modern lighting. When the lighthouse was saved in 1990 the people of Happisburgh felt there was a very real need for the light to be retained. At that time only large commercial vessels had expensive electronic satellite equipment. Today it is possible to get satellite navigation and GPS via a mobile phone, so just about all boats on the water carry some degree of electronic aid. Large commercial vessels are still obliged to carry paper charts and have an officer on board to navigate by them, just in case their electronic systems fail. The role of the lighthouse has now become a secondary role – thus if that singled-handed yachtsman, small fishing vessel, coastal freighter or cruise liner gets into difficulty, he knows that Happisburgh lighthouse will be there to guide and reassure him.

Happisburgh lighthouse undergoing repainting in 1907. (From the Neil Storey Archive)

Chapter 9

Education in Happisburgh

Education during the later part of the 18th century was provided for the able and those who could afford it. The oldest establishment, the Free Grammar School, was held in a pebble and thatch building not far from the church and known for many years as Tithe Barn. Its most illustrious pupil was Richard Porson, son of Huggin Porson, worsted weaver and parish clerk in the neighbouring village of East Ruston. Richard was a promising scholar who soon outshone his fellow pupils. He composed verses, one of which, written when he was eleven, commemorated the wreck of *HMS Peggy*. Another of his early efforts was inspired by a moonlight night:

> Who can the beauties of the night describe
> When the bright moon and all the starry
>   tribe
> Emit their splendour when the day is done.
> Those brilliant orbs succeeded one by one.
> Who can consider this but for an hour
> And not be astonished at the Almighty
>   power.
> With how much regularity they're made
> And with such beauty as will never fade.
> Then cease, vain man, thine own vain works
>   to prize
> Consider what is placed in the skies.
> If thou thy study unto this should turn
> A lesson in humility thou'st learn.

His early promise was noted by the Reverend Thomas Hewitt, Perpetual Curate of Walcott, who taught him with his own sons the rudiments of Latin and Greek, and it was as a classical scholar and not as a poet that he made his name. Through Mr Hewitt's commendation he was sent to Eton by Mr John Norris of Witton Park, the founder of the Norrisian Professorship of Divinity at Cambridge. From there he entered Trinity College in 1778, gaining a fellowship when he was only 22 years of age. This he relinquished later, having decided against taking Holy Orders, but was appointed Regius Professor of Greek. He added greatly to the knowledge of metre, Greek idiom and usage, and among his best known works are his editions of Aeschylus and Euripedes. Sadly, he was an alcoholic, and in later life extolled the virtues of small beer rather than the moon:

> When wine is gone and ale is spent,
> Then small beer is most excellent.

When intemperance caused his death in 1808 at the age of 49, he was buried in the ante-chapel of Trinity College. The brief inscription on the paving stone marking his grave gives little indication of his achievements and no hint of his tragic end, but high above, looking down from the row of plaster busts lining the chapel walls, is his sad and dissipated face.

In 1770, another school, built by subscription, was opened at the southern end of Whimpwell Green for the children of Happisburgh and Lessingham. Later, in 1803, when much of the remaining open and waste land was enclosed, three roods of common land were allotted to the school, for which Thomas Lloyd, then Vicar and patron, paid the Commissioners' expenses of £5-0s-5d. For 61 years Robert Summers was the master there, working for a salary of £10 a year plus the penny or two each pupil brought weekly. It was to him that the Vicar, the Reverend Theophilus Rice, left his treasured copies of *Tatler*, *Spectator* and *The Guardian*. He appears to have had complete charge of the school from its opening until his death at the age of 83, when his son claimed both building and land as private property.

Not all school masters were so dedicated to their profession. Thomas Clarke, one of Mr Summers' successors, gave it up to become landlord of the Swan Inn and 'mail contractor' with land surveying and tax collecting as sidelines. The school building eventually fell into disrepair, and by the mid 1860s there was only one school in the village.

This was the Church of England or National School which replaced the Free Grammar School in 1811 and occupied the same building. Girls as well as boys whose parents could afford to pay a few pence a week were admitted. Several poor children received free education through the bequest of the Revd Jonathan Challoner who had directed that £6 be used annually for this purpose. The increased number of pupils could no longer fit comfortably into the small and unsuitable building, so in 1861 'a large and handsome red brick structure of Gothic architecture' was erected at a cost of more than £600.

This sum was raised partly by public subscription and partly by a government grant. There was said to be accommodation for 140 children although the average attendance was 95.

A succession of single ladies ran the school, assisted by a pupil teacher and a monitor. Life for the village schoolmistress was hard. All children above infant age were herded into the larger of the two rooms, the older boys were frequently troublesome, the fires smoked in windy weather, and over all hung the dreaded annual visit and report of Her Majesty's Inspector. The financial state of the school and the mistress' professional reputation depended on the result of the examination he conducted. If the work and discipline failed to reach the high standard required, the Merit Grant (a Government grant) would be reduced or withdrawn. The Inspectors, who were ordained priests, appear to have taken little account of limited ability, for except in extreme cases of mental deficiency, all pupils were expected to reach the same standard.

However, the Reverend James Slater, vicar of Happisburgh, took a very great interest in the school throughout the 36 years of his incum-

An early view looking south along the main street through the village. Mrs Hannant's shop is on the right, with the village school beyond. The bell, which called pupils in to lessons, can be seen hanging in the small turret between the two chimneys.

bency. He paid frequent visits to teach scripture and arithmetic, dealt with a difficult pupil and was always ready to give advice when asked. His wife and daughter often helped with singing and needlework. It was the custom for the ladies of the village to provide material which when made up would be returned to the donor. Several girls could be kept busy working on one calico night shirt, learning to make buttonholes and hem with almost invisible stitches. It was of little consequence if they found the work monotonous. Knitting was introduced into the curriculum in 1869 for both boys and girls. The former were much interested, but became 'rather disorderly disputing over their knitting pins'. In an emergency the Vicarage family would take charge of the entire school. Miss Eliza Slater was much concerned with the children's health. She sent soup to whooping cough sufferers, and during the scarlet fever epidemic of 1886 distributed leaflets 'on the containing of the disease' to all the children.

Absenteeism was a problem. Apart from illness – and epidemics of smallpox, scarlet fever and measles were recurrent and claimed their victims – wet weather, snow, chilblained feet and lack of boots prevented many from attending. Then there were the seasonal tasks needing child labour: turnip thinning, haymaking, shrimping, potato and acorn picking. At any time of year a wreck off the coast meant that wood and coal might be washed ashore, and this too was collected by some of the children during school hours. Late arrival was sometimes caused by taking breakfast to father who began his farm work at an early hour. A fine of five shillings could be demanded by the Parish Officer from parents of an absentee child. Pupils could leave school at the age of thirteen, or earlier if the required standard was attained.

The summer holiday was governed by harvest. After the wet August of 1879 School did not close until 14 September, and when it reopened five weeks later, many children stayed in the fields gleaning. In the early days of the

The pupils of Happisburgh school in a photograph taken in 1894.

The pupils of Happisburgh school in a photograph taken about 1905. The man at the right-hand end of the middle row is the then headmaster Mr Barnes, while the older boy at the left-hand end of the same row is his stepson.

The infant pupils of Happisburgh school in a photograph taken about 1905. The woman at the right-hand end of the row is Miss Bessy Thompson. The woman on the left is unknown, and Mrs Barnes stands behind her.

National School, Easter was not always marked by even a day's holiday, but a half day was taken for Shrove Tuesday, and Ingham Fair on Trinity Monday was never unobserved. Often School was closed for the whole week, for the Fair moved to Hasbro' Hill on Trinity Tuesday. A week was usually taken at Christmas too, and during the last week of the autumn term the infants joined the older pupils in the larger room so that their class room could be given over to the making of Christmas decorations for the church. This was done by the monitress and some of the older children making long ropes of evergreens to drape round the pulpit, font and screen. There were also occasional holidays – a whole day in summer for boys in the church choir when Mr Slater took them to Hickling or Cromer, and for the whole School when the building was required for confirmation candidates. And there were national events to be commemorated. The Queen's Jubilee in 1887 was celebrated by a whole day and a half's holiday. Miss Slater had practised the National Anthem and other suitable songs with the children in anticipation of this. A half day was given in March 1900 in honour of the Relief of Ladysmith and another in May for the Relief of Mafeking. The vicar, now the Reverend Hitchcock, provided tea to mark the former occasion in the newly built Slater Memorial Church Room.

Miss Elizabeth 'Bessy' Thompson (1876–1958)
When little Bessy Thompson first went to school as a small child in 1881 there were just two rooms, the 'big room' in front, running the length of the building and a smaller one at the back for the infants.

The schoolmistress, Miss Harriet Ducker, who was in charge of about ninety children, was assisted by a pupil teacher, a monitor and a monitress, two of the older pupils. After daily instruction from Miss Ducker, these two passed on the information to groups of younger children. Learning was by rote and very repetitive. Miss Ducker was a disciplinarian, and not well liked. When she married a lighthouse keeper and departed to the Scilly Islands, there was

rejoicing on her wedding day for more reasons than one.

In 1889 Bessie was appointed monitress and received a small payment. One of her duties was to pull the bell rope to summon pupils into school. The bell was hung in a small turret above the porch, and could be heard at a considerable distance by late-comers as well as those already in the playground. The next stage in Bessy's progress was to become a pupil teacher. She was expected to arrive at 8.00am for instruction in teaching the lessons set for the day and to further her own education. As the yearly examination by one of Her Majesty's Inspectors proved satisfactory, she received a government grant and completed the five-year apprenticeship. Although not obtaining a place at training college, she was given the post of assistant teacher.

From then on and through the first three decades of the 20th century, Miss Bessy Thompson reigned supreme in the Infant Room. There were changes. The large photograph of Queen Victoria gave place to that of the reigning monarch, a piano replaced the harmonium and the children sat on small chairs instead of long benches. On top of a glass-fronted cupboard was a stuffed barn owl, and within, amid a collection of natural and man-made objects, was an ostrich's egg and a small toy monkey dressed in a red jacket. This was Miss Thompson's property and only came out on very rare occasions as a special treat. Below were piles of slates, boxes of chalk and dog-eared spelling books and reading primers. The alphabet and 'The cat sat on the mat' were inscribed in large letters on a banner of American cloth hanging on the classroom door.

The only form of heating was an open fire which smoked when the wind was in the wrong direction. In wet weather steam arose from the wet clothes drying on the guard, for everyone walked to school, whatever the weather. Some children brought a potato to be baked on the trivet for their dinner. Every year, just before 'Stir up Sunday (the last Sunday before Advent), Miss Thompson asked the children to bring the ingredients for a Christmas pudding. This was

The pupils of Happisburgh school posing outside the Church Room in 1908.

made under her supervision, and each child would be allowed a 'stir' before it was put in a cloth and boiled over the classroom fire. There was much excitement when the steaming pudding was ready and everyone had a taste.

During the Spring term of 1932 Miss Bessy Thompson became unwell and retired at Easter, having spent over 50 years of her life at Happisburgh School. She died in 1958 at Easter time at the age of 82.

Extracts from the School Logbooks

14 January 1863: Much confusion caused in the 3rd Class by Robert Clipperton, punished the latter, but afterwards found that Robert Ducker had brought the stones into school.

11 February 1863: Very disorderly throughout the day, endeavoured to discover the cause, found it arose in the morning from some boys having concealed dead mice in their pockets. Offenders kept in till 6:30pm.

19 May 1863: Spoke to 1st Class on necessity of paying respect to 'age'. Learnt texts on subject.

15 June 1863: Left school from 10–11:15 owing to the sudden indisposition of Alice Cutting ... on returning, spoke to children on the illness and expected death of their school fellow – many of the girls much affected.

26 June 1863: Children's attention arrested and voluntary silence throughout the school by the bell tolling for the death of Alice Cutting.

27 July 1863: Girls commenced four Night Shirts for Mrs Wilkinson.

30 July 1863: Finished the 4 Shirts.

4 October 1863: Mr Slater spoke to R. Clipperton of his mischievous conduct with Books.

29 June 1869: Boys rather disorderly in afternoon disputing over their knitting pins.

1 July 1869: Boys much interested in their knitting. Ten can do the plain stitch fairly well.

15 October 1869: Miss Slater taught a new school song tune – *Auld Lange Syne*.

20 June 1870: Commenced making ten grey calico garments.

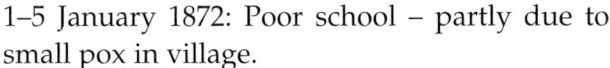

1–5 January 1872: Poor school – partly due to small pox in village.

15 July 1872: Boys wanted for carrying of the hay.

26 April 1875: Another child – Sarah Bronwick – died of scarlet fever. (Seven children died during this epidemic.)

14 October 1878: Several older children absent picking acorns.

19–23 May 1879: Several children absent this week shrimping.

14–18 July 1879: Many children absent turnip-picking.

23 November 1880: Usual order of lessons interrupted by Duke of Edinburgh passing through village. Children cheered him as he passed.

22–23 June 1887: Wednesday and Thursday a.m. Holiday to celebrate Queen's Jubilee.

17–21 December 1887: Older children and monitress engaged in helping with Church decorations. Class Room given up for this work.

15 April 1889: Bessie Thompson commenced as paid Monitress.

3 October 1890: Little Martha Thomspon badly fractured her thigh, she has to lie in bed five weeks. Alice Thompson aged 13 kept at home in consequence.

14 November 1890: Lydia Cutting away – no boots.

4 October 1891: Opened School after five weeks and one day extra due to New Class Room not being finished.

13 June 1893: Edwin Smith, 13 years, left to serve a Thatcher.

6 July 1893: Half Holiday given on the occasion of the marriage of the Duke of York.

16 May 1895: Children attended Mr Slater's funeral at 12pm.

2 March 1900: Half holiday given in afternoon in honour of the Relief of Ladysmith and our victory over Crongi the Boar (*sic*) Leader. The Vicar kindly gave tea to all the scholars in the Church Room.

21 May 1900: Half Holiday to commemorate the Relief of Mafeking.

The School Today
In 1938, all children, at the age of eleven, moved to the new Secondary Modern School at Stalham, or to Paston Grammar School or the Girls' High School at North Walsham. Happisburgh was then known as a primary school. Happisburgh School became a First School in 1980, taking children aged four to eight years, who then moved on to Stalham Middle School.

Extensive building work was completed in 2005, enlarging the School considerably. There are now five classrooms, one of which is used by pre-school children, and a hall. Once again it is a Church of England Primary School with a wide catchment area and an attendance of 100 children. Long gone are the days of learning by rote and a narrow curriculum. Today, Spanish and French are on the syllabus, and after-school activities include archery and capoeira, unheard of in Victorian times.

Chapter 10

Agriculture in Happisburgh

Arthur Young, in his work entitled *General View of the Architecture of the County of Norfolk*, which was drawn up for the consideration of the Board of Agriculture and published in 1804, thought that Happisburgh, Walcott and Bacton had 'the finest soil, perhaps, in the county: a rich, deep mellow, friable loam on a clay loam bottom, some on brick-earth and sand; all good.' In 1800, land near Happisburgh was selling at £30 or £40 an acre, but the best land in the village made £50 an acre. The farms in this area generally varied in size between 50 and 300 acres, but the majority of the villagers kept a few pigs, poultry and perhaps a cow, and grew fodder for their livestock.

The Farming Year

The farming year traditionally began in October, on Michaelmas day, 10 October. Many farm tenancies changed on this day, and a lot of farm workers moved jobs. The year began with ploughing. In Norfolk the ploughmen were

This photograph from the 1950s shows Jim Prior from Sloley who took a percheron stallion around to farms to mate with mares. He is shown holding Rodney Mason – Jim stayed with Rodney's parents when in Happisburgh.

called teamsmen, and they all took great pride in their horses and were responsible for their welfare. The head teamsman was the senior man on the farm.

Boundaries were also maintained at this point of the year. Hedges were 'layed', i.e. cut back and woven to form stock-proof barrier, using a Norfolk pattern billhook and a dannock (a thick leather glove). Ditches were dug or re-dug and drains were laid. Drains were paid for in 22-yard lengths measured out with a chain and clay pipe field drains were introduced in the late 18th century.

In the autumn, the ploughed land was harrowed and rolled and the broadcast sowing of wheat began, generally in the middle of October, and continued to December, sometimes until Christmas. Winter wheat was sown from horse-drawn drills, and if a small patch was missed, it was re-sown with a small hand drill or 'dodgers'. Diddling, when practised, began at Michaelmas. Three or four seeds were put in each hole, two inches deep, as is explained in a local verse:

> One for the rook, one for the crow.
> One to rot and one to grow.

The average yield from Happisburgh's wheat-fields was 9 coombs an acre, compared to Honing's average of 7 coombs an acre and North Walsham's 6 to 7 coombs.

The autumn also saw the root crops – swedes, turnips and mangolds – lifted for animal feed. These were stored in 'hales' or 'clamps' (heaps) and were covered with straw or kept under cover. Cattle were moved into the yards, and the teamsmen and cowmen were often expected to look after the health of animals. Over the winter

A view of one of Happisburgh's farmyards taken in the 1890s, showing the haystacks, carts and other paraphernalia of the harvest.

months, root crops were mechanically cut up to provide animal feed. Oil cakes, made from linseed or cotton seed, were also fed to the animals during the winter.

Threshing started in December and continued into January. It was the first of the intensive jobs to be mechanized, and by the 1920s was mostly undertaken by contractors moving from farm to farm, pulling the threshing drum and elevator behind a steam traction engine. These teams worked up to 15 miles from their home base, and the driver and his mate took bicycles to ride home at night.

Lambing started in January and continued well into the spring. The shepherd would often live with the flock in moveable wooden hut, sleeping on a straw-stuffed sack with a pen for weak lambs beneath the bed. His hut would also have a cast-iron stove for heating and cooking, and a medicine cupboard.

February often also saw the rat-catcher at work. Rats and mice invaded barns to feed on corn and roots. All farms had semi-wild cats fending for themselves, occasionally being given a saucer of milk at milking time. Tunnelling moles could also cause damage to crops and pastures, and mole-catchers used homemade traps and poisons to catch and kill them. Rooks and crows were scared off growing crops by children with rattles.

Ploughing took place throughout January and February, and was followed in March by the drilling and sowing of crops. The seed was broadcast with a 'small-seed' drill, which was much wider than a corn drill. Small areas could be sown with a 'fiddle drill', by hand casting or from a hand barrow. The newly cast seed was then lightly covered with soil using a set of wooden harrows. By the time the corn was well up in May, the thistles needed to be weeded out from among the crop. Barley was sown from February to April, and in Happisburgh and Walcott a yield of 14 coombs an acre was expected, much higher than elsewhere. For malting, an unsheaved scythed crop turned over for two or three days in sunny weather gave good results. Oats were sown in Spring, using five bushels an acre of broadcast seed. When drilling was used, which in Happisburgh was not until the 19th century, only half of that quantity of seed was required.

Arthur Young recorded that beans were being grown by Mr Wiseman of Happisburgh in the late 18th century, although they were not being grown elsewhere in the district at that time. The seed was sown by hand in every other furrow, and the ground was hand-hoed twice. The crop yielded 14 or 15 coombs an acre, and was used for fodder. Peas were also grown for fodder, dibbling was often used and the crop was not hoed. White clover was thought to make the best hay. Mr Wiseman apparently sowed 19 pounds of seed per acre (the normal quantity was 12 pounds) and he could cut two wagon-loads from each acre. Rye-grass and vetches were also sown for hay. Buckwheat, a member of the dock and knotgrass family, was fed green to sheep and the seeds were cracked to provide fodder for cows, horses and pigs. The seeds, like miniature beech nuts, were sown from mid-May to early June.

In June the hay was harvested – a vital winter food for horses, cattle and sheep. The cut grass was turned with wooden rakes and forks and stacked in haycocks to dry before carting in a 'morphrey' – a wheeled platform added to an ordinary cart to increase loading capacity.

A team of horses pulling a binder during the harvest. Before, and even after, the introduction of mechanised farming, horses were crucial to the successful running of a farm.

This photograph taken about 1900 shows agricultural labourers visiting Happisburgh forge to get their tools sharpened before the harvest.

Shocks of corn ready to be collected by the harvest wagon in the 1930s.

Harvesting of the barley, oats and wheat began in August and continued into September. During the harvest workers arrived at the field at 6am, the mowers with their scythes and rubs (sharpening stones). Whole families would come to the harvest, bringing food to supplement any food and drink that the farmer supplied. The harvesters moved forward in an oblique line mowing the crop, taking their time from the leader. Each man was followed by two women who gathered up the corn and tied it into small sheaves.

By the 1920s, men cut the harvest with horse-drawn reapers and binders, using scythes to make way for the machines. Women followed the reaper to tie up sheaves and stand them up in 'shocks' to dry.

A team of men followed them shocking (stooking) the corn, ready to be collected by the harvest wagon. Each harvest wagon had a 'holdger-boy', a lad who sat on the back of the horse and was responsible for driving the wagon from shock to shock. Every time he was about to move, he yelled 'Holdger!', warning the men on the load to hold tight. When the last load had been gathered, it was a Norfolk custom for the pitcher to pick up the holdger-boy by putting the tines of his pitchfork under the boy's arms and pitch him up on to the load, from there he rode to the barn. Once back at the farmyard, the corn was stacked in the farmyard and thatched to keep out rain. Once the work was done, the harvest supper was held amid much rejoicing.

In September, the potatoes were lifted, most often by female workers, and the harvest supper was provided by the farmer for all of the workers. With the extra money eared during the

Hay stacked in the fields near the lighthouse before being collected and taken back to the farmyard.

Carting wheat at Hill Farm with Mr Turner on the tractor.

George Williamson, Edna Whitwood and Alice Winn picking potatoes up by hand.

harvesting, rents were paid and a few new clothes and boots bought at harvest sales in town. Harvest thanksgiving services were held in the local churches and the whole cycle began again for another year.

Agricultural Workers

In some parts of the Happing Hundred two shillings a day were paid to labourers in winter and summer alike. A lump sum of £2-12s-6d was paid for harvest, with board. At Horning, the winter rate was 1s-4d or 1s-6d and the summer rate 2s, and wheat could be bought by the men at a reduced price of 5s a bushel. At North Walsham, according to Arthur Young, the wages were as follows: in 1752, one shilling and three pints of good strong beer a day; in 1772, one shilling and two pints of tolerable good beer; and in 1792 one shilling in the winter, 1s-2d in the summer and one pint of miserable small beer.

Isaac Crow was an agricultural labourer, as were most of his neighbours. When the long day spent working for his master was over, he cultivated the land he rented, and for this purpose owned a plough, a cart, a pair of harrows and a

mare. Two or three cows provided milk and cheese, the latter being made during the summer, and stored in an upper room for use throughout the winter. Here too were tubs filled with salted pork. Two pigs would be kept to provide for the future, but the surplus were killed at Martinmas. Before the introduction of root crops, the larger part of the herds of cattle and pigs were butchered at the onset of winter. During the autumn, the children collected acorns and beech masts to supplement the pigs' diet. Although Isaac could not afford a bullock, he kept a few geese which provided the family with eggs and a good meal at Michaelmas.

The cottage was meagrely furnished: a bed in the parlour and another in the kitchen (where there was also the luxury of a warming pan), three tables, four chairs and a form, two pewter dishes and four plates. The family's few clothes were kept in a chest and a trunk. When Isaac was buried early in January 1714, just six months before Queen Anne, it was estimated that the contents of his cottage and yard were worth £19-12s-6d (NRO DN/INV 71/265).

But the value of a man's possessions was not necessarily an indication of his status in the village. Four years later, when James Heasleton, a yeoman, died, his goods and chattels were estimated at only seven shillings more than Isaac's (NRO DN/INV 74A/78). Of course, James farmed some acres of his own, but the apprisers included neither the land nor house in the probate inventory. Also, at 74, he was elderly, as were his two cows and much that he possessed and he was no longer able to farm as he once had done. Apart from five skeps of bees, he kept no more livestock during the winter than Isaac, but there was a bullock-house which he had no doubt used in earlier days. Beer was brewed in the baking house, although the copper, kettles and malt querns for grinding the barley were all now very old. Whereas Isaac kept his winter stores in an upper room, James' farmhouse had a dairy for the tubs of salt meat and the cheeses.

His most valuable possessions were in the house. The kitchen, which contained one of the three beds, was well provided with jacks, spits, grilling irons, pewter dishes and plates. There were bellows to start the fire, and two guns, perhaps used to provide rabbits for the pottage pots. A rather unexpected item was a looking glass, but James's wife must have spent much of her time in the kitchen, and it was certainly the most used room in the house. The linen included a tablecloth and eight napkins – articles unknown to households such as Isaac Crow's or Samuel Keeler's. James also owned a few special treasures in silver – a tobacco box, a small cup, two spoons, and a taster.

Three Happisburgh Farmers

During the 1720s farming in Happisburgh as elsewhere, began to undergo significant changes. The old method of two- or three-year crop rotation had been used by the Heasletons, Middletons and the rest for generations, providing wheat, oats and rye for bread, barley for malt, and leaving some land fallow each year. But Robert Brown, yeoman, was ready to try new ideas. Turnips had been grown extensively at Raynham by Lord Townsend to provide an addition to hay as winter fodder for the farm stock, and Robert gave over 18 acres to the crop. He found that with 12 acres of buckwheat he could feed his seven cows, keep back a number of the yearling cattle from the Martinmas slaughtering, and still have sufficient for his large flock of sheep. During the summer he kept between 80 and 90 ewes and lambs. He also had about a dozen horses, a number of pigs and fowls in the yard.

Robert Betts, a husbandman or tenant farmer, needing more hay than he could cut from the permanent pasture and waste space land, sowed clover and 'darnel seed' for that purpose. The use of 'darnel' is puzzling, for it is a poisonous grass – the 'tares' of the New Testament. However, as the word 'tares' was synonymous with 'vetch' it would appear that Robert was following the practice of drying vetches for winter use. He needed to fill his barns, for he overwintered thirty cattle, eleven horses and the same number of cows and pigs. The hay was supplemented with buckwheat, a plant of the dock family, which gave a crop of seed like miniature beech masts. When cracked, these provided food for all of the animals.

Of greater standing in the village than either the

husbandman or the yeoman, was Thomas Faulke, gentleman. He grew a small quantity of turnips for his herd of twenty cows and a bull, but like Robert Betts, he was old-fashioned enough to rely largely on his barns of hay. Thomas lived in a comparatively large and well furnished house. The parlour contained several cane chairs and a corner cupboard for china, while in the study he kept his bureau, books, pistols and swords. All the principal rooms had looking glasses, and there were closestools (night-commodes) in two bedrooms. Spice drawers, a coal-cradle and smoothing Irons were also in his possession. He had 6 horses to work the land, to ride and to draw the chaise. At his death in 1731 his total assets were £568 14s 6d (NRO DN/INV 79A/24).**f**

Robert Brown, although a little lower in the social scale of village life, was climbing rapidly upwards. In company with Thomas Faulke, he owned a watch and rings, but his clothes were more expensive than Thomas'. His wife served tea in china cups on a tray in the parlour, covering the table with a good linen cloth and providing her guests with napkins. Robert could read and write (his father Francis had been churchwarden on a number of occasions) but perhaps he did not value greatly the old books which were kept in the kitchen. Here too, were his two firelocks, a clock and a plentiful supply of domestic equipment. At his death in 1730 his possessions were valued at £590-9s-5d (NRO DN/INV 78B/47).

Robert Bett's house was quite well furnished with five ground floor rooms and five above, but the kitchen was the most important room. He had not changed from the habit of genera-tions of sleeping in the parlour, and using the parlour chamber, or room above, as a store for his wife's cheeses, and the clover and darnel seed. A looking glass was kept in the room above the kitchen. Apart from farming, he also took his turn to serve as churchwarden and had an interest in the village brick kiln, for bricks were replacing pebbles as a building material in Happisburgh. At his death in 1729, he owned 30,000 bricks and tools belonging to the trade, with assets totalling £503-19s-6d (NRO DN/INV 78A/10). In his will, Robert left £70 to his eldest son 'for the binding of him to a trade', £60 to his second son and the rest to his wife in trust for his youngest. (NRO NCC Will Register Rudd 52).

Happisburgh Mill
by Alison Yardy (Norfolk Historic Environ-ment Service)

Happisburgh Mill (NHER 11877), at Mill Farm, was built in 1773 to replace an earlier post mill that had been destroyed in the storm of 19 December 1770. Photographs of the mill in its working days show that it had the very unusual feature of twin fantails (the post mill at Hoveton was probably the only other example in Norfolk). These would have allowed the mill to pick up even the slightest change in wind direction. The eight-bay double-shut-tered patent sails powered three pairs of millstones – two pairs of French Burr stones for flour production and one pair of peak stones for crushing animal feed. The white painted weath-erboarded body or 'buck' was extended and fitted with a full-width decorative porch of a type distinctive to the east of Norfolk. The extension is likely to have been for the third pair of stones or perhaps to accommodate a flour dresser in response to the demand for white flour.

The mill was owned as part of a small farm. The acreage was reduced during the 19th century, but was recorded at 70 acres in 1851. Ownership passed from the Harvey family in the late 18th and early 19th centuries to their relatives, the Frareys by 1836. Thomas Harvey Frarey is recorded as miller and farmer here for more than 30 years. Happisburgh census returns generally show two employees associated with

This post mill at Mill Farm replaced an earlier once destroyed during a violent storm in 1770. Happisburgh Mill was unique in having two fantails instead of one; their function was to revolve the whole body of the mill into the wind. (Image courtesy of Norfolk County Council Library and Information Service)

the mill – a journeyman miller and a carter. The journeyman millers were employed to carry out the day-to-day operation of the mill. Miller's names recorded include James Ford in the 1820s, John Rayner between 1841 and 1854 and John Halls in 1861.

Thomas Harvey Frarey died in 1869 and for the next 20 years the farming and milling business was continued by his widow Mary. Eldred Porrett, who had previously worked at the tall tower mill in Hickling, was engaged as miller and is recorded here on both the 1871 and 1881 census returns. On Mary's death in 1889, the mill and farm, then with 39 acres, were offered for sale. The farming and milling business appear to have separated after this time with Arthur George Bates taking over the mill. The whole was offered for sale once again in 1893 and, as well as the mill and house, included walled-in flower and kitchen gardens, a small orchard, a three stall riding stable and coach house with granary and hayloft over. Mill Farm was then taken on by Arthur George Gibbs (who lived at Hall Farm) followed by the Gooch family by 1904. Arthur Bates continued with the milling business aided by steam power and helped by his son Arthur who carried on using steam power alone in the 1920s.

The windmill is believed to have been dismantled in 1921. By 1934 when photographed by H.E.S. Simmons, only the brick roundhouse remained with roof and a door intact. In 1937, when the remains were recorded by artist Karl Wood as part of his ambition to paint every windmill in Britain, only the walls of the roundhouse remained.

Livestock

Most households kept a few pigs to provide fresh, cured and salted meat. Arthur Young described how 'Mr Wiseman, at Happisburgh, having occasion to wean some pigs much too young, from the death of a sow ... tried boiling pease for them, and the success was so great, that he would never enter largely into breeding or fattening hogs without a furnace and copper for boiling whatever corn may be given.'

The most common bullock reared in Norfolk was the Galloway Scot, often bought at the Norwich market. Until the end of the Second World War, animals bought at Norwich on a Saturday were delivered to their purchasers on Sunday morning by a drover, one Mr Beales, who walked from farm to farm, reaching Lessingham by lunch time, when there was much excitement to see the new arrivals. Once fattened, farmers walked their cattle to St Faith's, near Norwich, and the drovers took them on to Smithfield in London. They would set out on a Sunday, arriving the following Sunday, ready for the Monday market. At Mile-End the salesmen met the drovers and took charge of their lots. It was the drovers' responsibility to take the money back to the farmers. In about 1844, cattle began to be taken to London by rail, arriving in a fresh condition. The increased expense of rail travel over droving was covered by the higher prices received for the fresh cattle. In fact, the farmers were said to have gained about £1 per head. During this period some 20,000 cattle were sent from Norfolk to Smithfield market each year.

John Millar (1852–1935)

During the Depression of the 1920s, many Scottish farmers moved to Norfolk to some of the best arable land in the British Isles, but they were preceded by John Millar from Nether Barr Farm in Ayrshire who made the journey in October 1885. John hired a train and loaded it with his dairy herd, the farm horses, crates of poultry, his plough, drill and binder, his carts and wagon, all his goods and chattels, his wife Annie, two small children and his mother and father. After a long and slow journey they alighted at Wroxham station. The horses were harnessed, the carts and wagon filled with family and possessions, while John and the cattle walked to Hall Farm in Belaugh. No doubt it took several trips before all was conveyed to their first Norfolk home.

By 1891, three more babies had arrived and the family moved again, a much shorter journey this time, to Lighthouse Farm in Happisburgh, where John stayed for the rest of his working life. The family grew in number to seven girls and three boys. Will, the eldest boy, enlisted in the 1914–18 War and sadly died of 'barbed wire poisoning'. Jim, although trained as a carpenter, took over Lighthouse Farm on his father's retirement. Don, the youngest son, bought Wyllie's Farm in Lower Happisburgh (now long gone) from his aunt, whose family had also travelled south, and in the late 1920s moved to Manor Farm, Lessingham, and later took over the adjoining Moat Farm as well. Although there were no grandsons to carry on the farming tradition, Jim's son, also named John, became a

Murray Ferguson with one of the Hasbro herd of Gloucester cattle.

vet specializing in farm animals, and so the link with the land remained for many years.

The Hasbro Herd of Gloucester Cattle
by Julia Ferguson

The Hasbro herd of Gloucester cattle was founded by Murray and Julia Ferguson in 1978. Murray had always been interested in old cattle breeds and, discovering that Gloucesters were dangerously near extinction with only 45 cattle left worldwide, decided to breed his own herd. The Gloucester cow is also noteworthy for its contribution to our medical history – it was the breed with which Edward Jenner discovered the smallpox vaccination in 1796.

The founding member was Bemborough Elijah, bred by Joe Hanson at the Cotswold Farm Park in Gloucestershire. He was joined by two cows, bought from the owners of some of the few remaining Gloucester cattle in the country.

They saw the value of a Norfolk herd should Foot and Mouth disease ever wipe out the last Gloucester cattle in the West Country. So Hasbro Annie and Hasbro Avril arrived in Norfolk – the Hasbro herd had been born.

Since 1978, the size of the herd has fluctuated, but increased steadily. By 2011, it numbered 32 animals and was one of the largest in the country. Most calves are fattened, mainly on home-grown and produced for beef. The occasional bull is reared and some heifers are kept for breeding.

Thanks to the interest of farmers across the country, the breed has now reached almost 100 animals. Gloucesters, which are chestnut in colour with a distinctive white finchback, or stripe, up their tail and spine, are dual purpose, providing both meat and milk. In demand once more for their excellent meat and cheese, their future is assured.

◇

Chapter 11

Happisburgh in the 19th–20th Centuries

Happisburgh has been a desirable seaside resort since at least the late 18th century, and continues to be so to this day, with many hundreds of people making their way to the coast to enjoy the sea views and home comforts offered by the village. Poets, artists, writers and actors visited and took inspiration from sandy shore, the crashing waves and the rugged scenery, while Bishops and Harley Street doctors stayed very happily year after year in cottages completely lacking in modem sanitation, undeterred by oil lamps and water from the well. Some visitors would opt for 'full board', but many brought in the ingredients for meals and handed them to the householder to be cooked on the kitchen range. Today, although some visitors stay at guest houses or the Hill House, many prefer to stay at the cliff-top caravan park.

Historically, one of the great attractions of Happisburgh was the opportunity for sea bathing which it offered. George IV's interest in sea bathing made it a popular pastime for the upper classes during the latter part of the 18th century, when, as Prince of Wales, he visited Brighton. Local entrepreneurs were quick to capitalise on this surge in interest, and the following advertisement appeared in the *Norwich Mercury* in June 1789:

> 'SEA-BATHING AT HAPPISBURGH ~ Benjamin Barrow respectfully informs the Public in general that he has erected a Bathing-Machine of the most approved Construction and provided proper Attendants for the Ladies and Gentlemen who may honour him with their patronage. The easy Declivity of the shore, the beauty of the surround-

One of the earliest incarnations of the cliff-top caravan park, seen here shortly after the Second World War, with the Hill House and the church in the background.

Hannant's Tea Gardens on the clifftops at Happisburgh, probably taken in the 1930s. The charabanc in the background would suggest a Sunday School outing visiting the village. The tea rooms were eventually relocated to The Street, next to the school.

Happisburgh beach has long been popular with those seeking to enjoy the sun, the sea and the sand.

Above left: *An early 20th-century photograph of a family enjoying the beach at The Gap. Note the lifeboathouse in the background at the top of the ramp down to the beach.* Above right: *Miss 'Dick' Whittleton and her cousin paddling off Happisburgh in 1912.*

ing country, and the convenient accommodations which Happisburgh can afford, are objects sufficiently important to attract the Attention of those who are in the Pursuit of Health and rural Enjoyment.'

Many of the old photographs of Happisburgh show temporary beach huts and tents erected seasonally at the foot of the cliffs for use by visitors and their families enjoying a day on the beach.

We are particularly fortunate in that a set of very early photographs of the village centre survive. During the 1980s the vicar received a surprise packet from one of Happisburgh's summer visitors who, on his return to the south coast, found an unexpected item in a second-hand book shop. It was a small hand-made case containing 14 faded sepia photo-

The ornate cover of the collection of late 19th-century photographs of the village now held in the church safe.

graphs of the village. They were undated, but a view of the church shows a barn on land where Albion Cottage and Church Cottage now stand. The cottages were built in 1893, proving that at least some of the photographs must precede this date. Among these images are the photographs of boats pulled up from the beach used as the frontispiece to this book, and the image of the farmyard used in the previous chapter, but many of the other photographs in the set show general views of the village and reveal a great deal about what has changed in the village and what has stayed the same.

The Millar girls bathing at Happisburgh in the 1920s.

The view north along The Street. The cottage on the left burnt down in the early years of the 20th century and was replaced by The Pightle. The thatched roofs of the two cottages next door – now Farthings – were also destroyed in the fire.

This photograph is taken from the North Walsham Road, looking east. The Hill House and the guesthouse next door can be made out at the back of the image, with cottages to the left of the frame and a range of low buildings to the right, including Tithe Barn. The cottages on the left of the road were demolished in the 1960s to make way for a garage, which has now also been replaced by three pleasantly designed houses.

A view of the church looking north from outside the school. Farm buildings can be seen occupying the site where Albion Cottage and Church Cottage now stand, indicating that this photograph at least must predate 1893.

A view south along Whimpwell Street. Lighthouse Farm – now known as Pebbles – looks little changed, but the pond was much larger. The farm was the home of the Millar family, hence the pond being known as Millar's Pond. The farm in the distance on the right-hand side of the road was replaced long ago with two cottages, and some of the farm buildings have been converted into dwellings.

The Hill House

In the 16th century, the Hill House originally comprised three Tudor cottages, which, in the 17th century were knocked through to become and ale house, and there are traces of brickwork from this period to be found in the building (NHER 18473). In the early years of the 18th century the inn, then known as the Windmill Inn, became a coaching inn on the coast route between King's Lynn and Great Yarmouth. The inn gained notoriety as being the haunt of smugglers and beachmen, and when the village mill blew down in 1770 the opportunity was apparently taken to rename the inn the Hill House instead. The large, three-storey guesthouse was built adjacent to the inn in around 1800, and the

The front of the Hill House and the adjacent three-storey guesthouse, as it would have first appeared to its many distinguished visitors.

The rear of the Hill House, which commands spectacular views of the sea. In the foreground is the highly thought of bowling green and a railway signal box built in anticipation of a railway that never came can be seen to the left of the frame.

stables were constructed to the rear in the 19th century. It is recorded that in 1879 the landlord purchased the wreck of the tug *Reliant* of Yarmouth, wrecked at Cart Gap, for building materials, although there are no obvious timbers from this visible except perhaps some of the floor boards.

In its time, the Hill House has attracted a great many famous visitors. The poet and hymn writer William Cowper visited Happisburgh twice in his last sad years when suffering from mental illness. In 1795 he walked along the beach from Mundesley with his cousin, the Reverend Dr John Johnson. Johnson's diary records the following entry (Spiller 1927):

'Aug. 31st, 1795. Walked to Happisburgh by the edge of the sea all the way. Dined in a Lodging House, where I borrowed a room for the purpose, to avoid the noise of the Public House and after dinner returned to Mundesley. This was the only instance of Mr Cowper's ever eating, as he told me afterwards, with anything like an appetite, in Norfolk; and to be sure, he did eat very heartily, though of very ordinary food, for the only things he would touch were

Beans and Bacon, which were very old, and apple pye, the worst I ever saw. He ate, however, with a most complete relish of them all. I never knew him to enjoy a dinner anything like it after that, to the day of his death.'

The pair visited Happisburgh again three years later:

'June 7th, 1798. I coaxed him to day into a boat in which he and I and our servant were rowed to Happisburgh. He went with me to see the Light House and appeared to enjoy in some measure looking thro' a telescope from that very lofty building, at the ships in the offing. After dining at the Public House on the Hill, we walked home – the sea being too rough for us to venture in the boat.'

Among other notable guests at the Hill House is Henry Irving, the 19th-century actor–manager of London's Lyceum Theatre and reputedly the inspiration for his personal assistant and theatrical manager Bram Stoker's novel *Dracula*. We know from Irving's letters

A signed photograph of Sir Henry Irving dedicated to Mrs Cubitt at the Hill House and dated 1898 (NRO MC1173/3).

that he holidayed at the Royal Links Hotel in Cromer the end of the theatrical season in August 1898, and it would seem that he visited or stayed at the Hill House. The Norfolk Record Office contains a handwritten letter from Irving to the then owner of the Hill House, Mrs Cubitt, dated 31st August 1898 which states: 'Many thanks for your kindness in returning the cigar cutter. Please give my special thanks to the little lady who found it.' The letter is accompanied by a signed photograph of the actor dedicated 'Mrs Cubitt from Henry Irving, 1898' (NRO MC1173/1–3).

Sir Arthur Conan Doyle visited the Hill House Hotel while on a motoring holiday in the county at the beginning of the 20th century. While he was staying in the hotel, the landlord's son Gilbert Cubitt showed him a signature he had developed using stick figures. This inspired Conan Doyle to write the Sherlock Holmes story *The Adventure of the Dancing Men*. In the story,

Holmes and Watson are called to Norfolk by Hilton Cubitt, the local squire, to investigate a mystery. Holmes eventually solves the case by cracking a code which consists of little dancing figures – like those of Gilbert Cubitt. Doyle also took the name Cubitt from his visit, and another local link is that, in the story, Cubitt lives in the village of Riding Thorpe – which is almost certainly a composite of local villages Ridlington and Edingthorpe. Conan Doyle may even have written the story in the Green Room of the old Boarding House which overlooked the bowling green.

Shopping in Happisburgh

During much of the 19th and early 20th centuries Happisburgh was almost self-supporting. The oldest business, still here today, is Wayside Stores and Post Office. For most of the 19th century and until the end of the First World War, Wayside Stores was owned by the Ducker family. David Frederick, always known as Fred, was the last of his line to be Postmaster, a position he held for 30 years or more. He was also a pork butcher, and as well as groceries, sold most things needed by village folk. Helen, his eldest daughter, had happy memories of her childhood and the shop:

'Ours was a general shop, pork butchers, drapery, boots and shoes, everything you can think of The Post Office came first and had a grill in front. Behind were shelves stocked with royal blue bottles containing potions and powders such as syrup of figs,

A view of Wayside Stores and the Post Office in 1902. Esther Ducker, aged four, stands in the doorway and her brother and sister, Charles and Helen, are by the gate.

Sir Arthur Conan Doyle was inspired to write the Sherlock Holmes story 'The Adventure of the Dancing Men' while staying at the Hill House. In 1984, the Sherlock Holmes Society of London visited the pub as part of a tour of East Anglian places with Holmesian connections.

The Hill House was not the only hotel in the village. The Swan Hotel, seen here, offered 'well aired beds, good stabling, and pony and trap hire' in the late 19th century. It closed in the 1960s. The Victoria, described as a beerhouse, stood in Lower Happisburgh and closed in the early 1990s.

The Post Office and General Stores when Mr Cyril Easlea was postmaster. The shop was demolished in the early 1960s and the Post Office returned to the Wayside Stores.

In the 19th and 20th centuries, many goods were sold from the backs of carts that visited the village.

tincture of rhubarb, dock for treating bruises, peppermint and lavender water. There were pig powders, soap and salts for sheep. Further on was the drapery; rolls of printed cotton, calico, towels, ribbons and bootlaces. Hanging from the ceiling were dustpans and brushes, scrubbing brushes and children's wooden spades and pails for the beach.

Groceries such as tea, coffee, rice and dried fruit were weighed and sold in bags of dark blue paper folded into shape by Mother. Sugar was cut from a large block, as was the cheese, and at the end of the counter stood a big coffee grinding machine. There were glass jars filled with sweets. Mother only had first class sweets, no common ones. She sold Peter's Milk chocolate, Fry's cream chocolate bars and Fry's assorted chocolates which came in ¼ pound boxes.

Behind the Post Office was the storehouse with the ironmongery, all in drawers from the ceiling to the ground. There were all sorts of nails and screws, hob nails and iron toe and heel plates. Children used to have thin irons screwed on to their boots because most of them had to walk so far to school. The soles of men's and boys' boots were covered with hob nails, all close together. They wouldn't have lasted five minutes on the roads otherwise.'

Wayside Stores and Post Office is still here today. The Post Office moved for a time to Mr Easlea's shop, a single-storey building nearer the church and now demolished, while just across the road Mrs Hannant was selling more groceries, ice creams, sweets and greengrocery. The Post Office returned to its original place in the 1950s. It is much smaller now, and no longer do we expect to buy pork, boots and dress material, but it is still a place where people stop and chat, and is much needed by the village.

In addition to the Wayside Stores, Mr Robert 'Schemer' Hemp in Camberley Cottage mended shoes and sold bicycles and paraffin, and at the other end of his house butchers from Stalham came over for two or three days each week. When Mr Hemp and his shop moved to a new bungalow, Bob took over from his father. He also made shrimping nets, beautifully crafted models of farm carts and gipsy caravans, and sold souvenirs for the holiday makers. Near by, during the 1939–45 War, sisters Doris Powles and Kathleen Hall kept a butcher's shop which after the war was moved to Beach Road.

In the early days milk was bought straight from the farm. It was often the children's job to take a tin can to be filled, and then carried carefully home before walking some distance to school. Later, the milkman brought churns round the village in a pony and trap. He carried a churn to the back door and ladled the milk out in a pint or half-pint measure into the householder's jug. Clifford Popay was a daily caller until the end of the last war. With the advent of pasteurisation and bottled milk a dairy run by Gerald Pestell, after his return from a Japanese Prisoner of War camp, and his wife Mary, was opened next to the butcher's in Beach Road, from where the milk was delivered by van.

The Frarey family had a bakery in Lower Happisburgh in the early days of the 20th century, and later Mr Jesse Gibson and his father were bakers on The Common at Aspen House, with Jesse travelling from door to door by van and carrying the loaves in a large basket. Stalham bakers visited the village for many years. Lower Happisburgh also had a flourishing Post Office and General Store (recently renamed Whimpwell Green Post Office), which did not close until 2005. In the 1930s and 40s Mr Burton, the postmaster and shopkeeper, also sold petrol from the first pump in the village.

When every farm kept horses, the blacksmith and saddler were much needed. John Thompson and his predecessors (also named John), ran the village forge for many years until his retirement during the 1940s. As well as the work of a farrier, there were scythes to be sharpened before haysel and harvest, ironwork for local builders, and much else, including fire-irons. John sometimes gave tongs, a poker and a shovel to a couple about to be married – a most useful gift when everyone had a coal fire. A saddler travelled from North Walsham to his small workshop in one of the Tithe Cottages for two or three days a week where he repaired and made harnesses and other leather goods.

Fish, freshly caught by the families of Cannon Harvey, Tom Lawson, Mrs 'Nellie' Grimmer and others was sold at the door. Lower Happisburgh also had a fried fish shop for many years. Today, a welcome addition to the village is a recently opened fresh fish shop where Bob Hemp once sold his shrimping nets.

Mrs Selina (Nellie) Grimmer (1865–1948) and her family

Like many Happisburgh folk in the 19th and early 20th centuries, George Grimmer spent most of his time fishing or working on the land. Living in Lower Happisburgh it was from Cart Gap that he set out in the *Shamrock*, or put out baited bank lines at low water from the shore, to be hauled up two hours after high tide. Crabs

George Grimmer

were plentiful in a good season from spring to early August, when they shed their shells and were said to have 'soft shell' and 'white foot'.

Then it was time to help with the harvest before the herring came down the coast in October. Cod and flat fish were there for the catching during the winter months. When George married Selina Harmer from Ingham he made a good choice. 'Nellie', as she was always known, was very hard working and used to village life. From then on, the White House in Whimpwell Green was her home. It was here that she brought up the surviving nineteen of her twenty-one children. Three of the eldest girls and one of the boys emigrated to the United States, and as 25 years separated the eldest from the youngest, it was always possible, as some moved on, to cram the remaining family into their three-bedroom cottage. Nellie chose some unexpected names for some of the children. There was John Augustus, Horatio Nelson (always known as 'Rasher'), Orlando Horace (nicknamed 'Pedro'), and Victoria 'Vicky' Roseanna.

Vicky left school when she was thirteen, and soon after went into service with a London family who moved in high society – they had once entertained Queen Mary to tea. Vicky stayed with the family for some years working as cook before returning to Happisburgh in 1924 to marry Edward Siely. She was never idle and could turn her hand to many things, from wallpapering to making clown dolls for charity, and caring for two of her brothers. As her daughter Helen said when she died aged 103, 'Her heart was in having bonfires and sawing and chopping wood'.

There was tragedy in the family, too. In October 1939, just six weeks after the outbreak of the Second World War, Rasher (Horatio) and Ike (Edward) went out for herring in the *Never Can Tell* with their friend Cecil 'Doley' Watts. Going through the breakers in a rough sea can be the most dangerous time. The boat overturned. Ike kicked off his boots and made for the shore, but Rasher and Doley drowned.

Nellie coped with the good and the bad alike. Through the years when the cottage was full of

Mrs Nellie Grimmer on her fish-cart.

children, she still found time to help with the fishing. Live crabs and lobsters were left on the cold stone floor of the larder for two days to 'clean themselves' before being cooked in the copper for 20 minutes. Much of the catch was sold by Nellie who went from door to door in a pony and trap, and it was she who called out members of the lifeboat crew when a ship was in trouble.

She was left a widow at the age of 63, but work continued. Some of the sons carried on with the fishing, and there was the five acres of land adjoining the cottage to be cropped and pigs to be fed. Although not well off herself, Nellie was always ready to help others. She never failed to slip in an extra fish for those of her customers who were finding life hard, and all who knew Nellie say that she had 'a heart of gold'.

Jonathan Balls, the Village Poisoner (1768–1845)

During the early years of the 19th century Jonathan Balls, a labouring man, and his wife Ann Elizabeth, six years his senior, lived in Lower Happisburgh, now known as Whimpwell Green. He was not well liked in the village, but showed much affection for his many grandchildren, and frequently had one or more staying in the cottage.

Death was never far away from large families when fever and smallpox were rife and medical knowledge limited. Although there was much sadness when little Maria Green died in 1835 while staying with Balls, her death was put down to 'the spotted fever'. Her five-year-old brother William also died while staying at Balls' cottage, and Martha, only thirteen months of age, died soon after a visit from Balls. All three children were violently sick and died a few hours later. They were buried at East Ruston where the Green family lived.

Suspicions were beginning to grow and rumours spread round the villages. Hannah Peggs, another grandchild, died in 1839, supposedly from smallpox, and her cousins Ann and Samuel Pestell died in 1843 and 1844 respectively. Then Balls' wife, who had been bedridden for several years, died aged 83 and was buried in Happisburgh churchyard on 4 January 1845.

In April, yet another grandchild, eight-months-old Elizabeth Pestell died. She was followed five days later by Jonathan Balls himself. Not long before, he told his daughter, Mrs Green, that 'death had struck him'. He asked for a piece of little Elizabeth's funeral cake and a glass of wine, saying that the rest could be saved for his funeral. He died at 3pm. All the deceased had died a few hours after suffering severe vomiting.

Public feeling became very strong, and although the parish authorities did not inform the Coroner, many villagers did. In response to their concerns, Mr Pilgrim, the County Coroner, ordered the bodies of Balls and Elizabeth Pestell to be exhumed and placed in a tent behind the church. Such a large crowd gathered that special constables were sworn in to keep order. An inquest was held at the Hill House on 19 April 1846.

The Jury were surprised to see two walking sticks in Balls' coffin, one on either side of the body, a poker, several handkerchiefs, some children's toys and a piece of plum cake in each of his hands. It was said that Balls, shortly before his death, had asked for these things to be buried with him. The handkerchiefs were his wife's and the toys had belonged to his granddaughter Elizabeth. Mr Clowes, a surgeon from Stalham, assisted by two other doctors, reported that there was enough arsenic in the two bodies to poison the whole parish.

The inquest was adjourned until the next day for the bodies of Mrs Balls and her grandchildren Ann and Samuel Pestell to be exhumed. All were found to have died from the effects of arsenic poisoning. Sarah Kerrison, a young servant girl who had cared for Mrs Balls for about five years, said that Balls made cold tea for his wife. He stirred it in one pot and poured it into another from which she drank from the spout. Shortly before Mrs Balls died, Sarah saw her husband drop two or three pinches of white powder into the pot. She thought this was some kind of remedy. William Pestell, father of Ann and Samuel, said he had been told that Balls bought arsenic from the Stalham druggist to kill rats. The Vicar, the Reverend Charles Birch, in reply to the Coroner, said that Balls was 'a very singular and cunning man' and he never had a good opinion of him. The Jury found that Jonathan Balls, his wife Ann, and Samuel and Ann Pestell had died from the effects of poison. There was no evidence to show how the arsenic was administered. It was impossible to say if the baby Elizabeth Pestell had suffered the same fate.

On 3 June 1846, at the insistence of the Secretary of State, an inquest was held on the bodies of Maria, William and Martha Green, the three children buried at East Ruston, and also of Hannah Peggs who had died seven years earlier at Ingham. All had been with or been visited by their grandfather and all had suffered from severe sickness shortly before they died. Once again the Jury found that all the deaths were caused by poisoning.

The Coroner noted that the finger of suspicion pointed at the deceased, Jonathan Balls, but he was beyond the reach of the law. It was regretted that an inquest had not been held immediately after the first death as it might have spared the lives of many. And so one of the most disturbing episodes in the life of Happisburgh folk ended, and one which would never be forgotten.

Wilfred Bion
by Sally Hardy

Born in India in 1897, where his family had long served, Wilfred Bion came to England to attend Bishop Stortford School in Hertfordshire. Many excursions were made to Happisburgh, for the School rented Church Farm, and arranged all year round trips for the boys. Swimming in the North Sea on high days and holidays, whatever the weather, became an important act of bravery and hilarity.

Wilfred excelled in sport of all kinds, which helped him integrate, for otherwise he was a

Church Farm was rented by the Old Stortfodians for use as a holiday home for many years until 1982. Henry Moore, Barbara Hepworth and Ben Nicholson stayed here in 1930 and 1931.

solitary boy with few close friends. School holidays not spent in Happisburgh would be with the Rhodes family at their Yorkshire farm, a descendant of whom is a resident of Happisburgh today.

The First World War was spent in action, and Wilfred's ability to understand and lead others helped save his life and the lives of many, but he felt saddened and demoralised by war. After the War he went to Oxford University to read History, and became intrigued and captured by Philosophy. His growing interest in psychoanalysis led his career to medical training at University College Hospital, London. The Second World War saw him as Senior Psychiatrist on the War Office selection board. Wilfred's understanding of people through his critical observations enabled him to influence how officers were trained and recruited. His group selection processes are still in use today, and could be said to have spawned the industry of adventure holidays and outward-bound courses as character-forming and team-building exercises. These experiences informed Wilfred Bion's future working life.

He worked at the Tavistock Clinic and eventually took over its chairmanship. He reformed the Clinic into its current role as an active and renowned leader in psychodynamic social psychiatry. With his leadership and insight into group psychotherapy the Tavistock became a highly successful and independent (self-financing) research institute. He has written numerous papers and is the author of fourteen books. He lived and worked in America (1968–79) and lectured internationally. He is recognised as one of the leading and most influential writers in the understanding of group psychotherapy.

Wilfred Bion always remained fond of Happisburgh and on his death in 1979 his wish to be buried in Happisburgh was honoured – a final resting place for the ashes of a man whose life could have taken him anywhere in the world. He chose a quiet spot, with breathtaking views of the sea, a representation in itself of a man whose self doubt failed to overshadow individual brilliance.

Village Events

As well as the demands of the agricultural economy and the need to earn a living, there has always been a very sociable side to village life, as is exemplified by the village's numerous sports teams, amateur dramatics productions, carnival, sports days, village fetes, scout troup and musical recitals, to name but a few. Many of

The cast of a local amateur dramatics production of The Mikado *in the early 1920s.*

A fairy-themed event being held at the Vicarage in around 1905.

the village activities were conducted in aid of the restoration of the churches in Happisburgh and Walcott. A large number of photographs of these events survive, although unfortunately they are not always accompanied by explanatory notes or lists of names. A selection of these photographs is reproduced here.

Sports have always played a large part in the social life of the village, and the village has produced a number of very successful football teams and cricket teams, some of whom are pictured here. Bowls, too, was very popular and the bowling green behind the Hill House was spoken of as a very fine example of the type. Part of the game's appeal was explained by Ernest Suffling: 'bowls … can be played by persons of any age and size, and without the slightest fatigue. For a portly gentleman of some sixty summers and 20 st, or a trifle more, in weight, cricket is out of the question; but a quart of 'Old Tom', as the best ale is here called, a yard of clay, and a four-handed game of bowls, will suit him admirably' (Suffling 1897, 174–5).

In 1909, Sir Ernest Shackleton, the Antarctic explorer, came to Happisburgh to give a lecture illustrated with lantern slides about the 1907–09

HAPPISBURGH & WALCOTT
Coronation Day Sports

PROGRAMME OF EVENTS.

	PRIZES IN CASH.	1st.	2nd.	3rd.
Three-legged Race (Girls)	... each	2/-	1/-	6d.
Three-legged Race (Boys)	...	2/-	1/-	6d.
Infants under 7, 50 yards	... ,,	1/-	9d.	6d.
Girls, 7 to 10, 100 yards	... ,,	1/-	9d.	6d.
Boys, 7 to 10, ,,	... ,,	1/-	9d.	6d.
Girls, 10 to 14, ,,	... ,,	1/6	1/-	6d.
Boys, 10 to 14, 200 yards	... ,,	1/6	1/-	6d.
High Jump (Boys)	... ,,	1/-	9d.	6d.
Thread Needle Race (Girls)	... ,,	1/-	9d.	6d.
Boys, 14 to 16, ¼-mile	... ,,	2/-	1/-	9d
Girls, 14 to 16, 200 yards	... ,,	2/-	1/-	9d.
Tug of War, Married v. Single (Ladies)	Winners 1/- each.			
Tug of War, Happisburgh v. Mr. Wenn's team. Prize given by Mr. Wenn, jun.				
400 yards Handicap (Men)	... each	3/-	2/-	1/-
Bolster Fight	... ,,	2/-	1/-	
100 yards Flat Race (Ladies)	... ,,	2/-	1/-	6d.
Sack Race (Men)	... ,,	2/-	1/-	6d.
Obstacle Race (Men)	... ,,	3/-	2/-	1/
Veterans' Race, over 65, 50 yards	,,	2/-	1/-	6d.
Veterans' Race (Ladies), over 65, 50 yards	,,	2/-	1/-	6d.
Boy Scouts, Donkey Polo	...	Prize given by Major R. B. Pearce.		
Tilting the Bucket	...	4/-		
Donkey Cart Race (2 up)	...	2/6 and 1 bushel Oats.		
Scouts' Tug of War	...	Winners, 6d. each.		
Men's Race, over 30, 100 yards	... each	2/-	1/-	6d.
Men's Race, over 50, ,,	... ,,	2/-	1/-	6d.
Blindfold Wand Race (Ladies)	... ,,	2/-	1/-	6d.

••••••••••••••••••

Adults' Sports, 2 to 3 p.m. Children's Sports, 3 to 4.
Pierrots, 4 to 5 p.m. Adult Sports, 5 to 7. Pierrots, 7 to 9.

••••••••••••••••••

"GOD SAVE THE KING."

D. M. Amiss, Printer, Market Street, North Walsham.

The programme for the Happisburgh and Walcott Coronation Day Sports event, marking the coronation of George VI in 1936.

The cast of a village concert party in the early 1950s, possibly held to mark the coronation of Elizabeth II.

The 'Band of Hope' temperance movement meets on Happisburgh beach, 1903.

The audience at one of the village concert parties held in the 1960s.

The cup-winning Happisburgh football team of 1911–12.

The Happisburgh Scout Troup with Major Pearce in 1913.

The Hill House Bowls Team in 1955. Back row (l–r): P. Gaul, C. Beane. P. Butler, H. Siely, A. Bates, E. French, J. Weddall. Front row (l–r): B. Hales, J. Hubbard, J. Siely, L. Watkins, W. Hannant.

Nimrod expedition to the South Pole. His was the first ship to winter in the Antarctic, and members of the expedition had walked further south than any previous expedition had achieved by that date. A large and enthusiastic audience gathered in the Church Room, which was, as the *Eastern Daily Press* reported, 'by dint of the utmost economy of space, was made to accommodate almost 200 persons'.

The Happisburgh Line

In 1897 the Great Eastern Railway (New Lines in Norfolk and Suffolk) Act was passed containing proposals to extend the existing Cromer to Mundesley railway line to Happisburgh, and the GER were considering further plans to extend the line all the way down the coast to Great Yarmouth. It was intended that the terminus would stand to the west of the school, providing easy access to the centre of the village and the clifftop. A similar scheme to bring the railway north from Great Yarmouth to Happisburgh was apparently also being considered under the terms of the Norfolk and Suffolk Joint Railway Act of 1898. A third proposal was apparently put forward by the Midland and Great Northern Joint Railway to extend their existing line from Stalham to Happisburgh, indeed there are photographs which show that a sign stating 'Stalham for Happisburgh and Palling on Sea' had already been erected at Stalham station in anticipation (Banyer and Clark 2003, 14).

These proposed extensions to the railway network go some way towards explaining the existence of one of the more intriguing buildings in Happisburgh – the railway signal box which stands in the garden of the Hill House Hotel (NHER 18473). This signal box was built in 1901 in anticipation of the arrival of the railway, although its signalling gear was never installed, and it was apparently rendered on the exterior in an Arts and Crafts style similar to that employed at Stalham station. For many years the signal box served as the tea room for the Hill House bowling club whose green lay in front of it, before eventually being converted for use as bed and breakfast accommodation for guests staying at the Hill House.

The signal box at the Hill House is not the only structure in the village to have been built in anticipation of the railways. A short terrace of four houses on Beach Road – Craigside, Cliff House, Sand Dune and Sunnyside – are often referred to locally as being 'railway cottages', although they weren't actually built by a railway company. These houses were built between 1901 and 1907 by an entrepreneur who had heard that the railway was coming to Happisburgh and who was keen to establish new boarding houses in anticipation of the rise in visitor numbers (Banyer and Clark 2003, 14). These four houses have survived for over a century, one pair of them fulfilling its intended role as a guest house for many years. In 2011 these houses were bought by North Norfolk District Council using funds from the Coastal Change Pathfinder Project with the intention of demolishing them to create a landscaped clifftop zone free from housing.

In anticipation of the coming of the railway, in the early years of the 20th century attempts were begun to turn Happisburgh into a 'seaside village of quality'. Plans were drawn up in 1908 by the architect C.E. Mallows of Hanover Square, London, showing the proposed development of the land to the west and north of the church, extending as far as Ostend Road, the boundary with Walcott, and to the clifftop. A spacious site was reserved for an hotel, 85 plots were designated for dwellings and formal landscaping was proposed from Blacksmith's Lane to Church Farm Corner. On the northern side of the church, public gardens would stretch to the clifftop (a cold and windswept spot!) and a golf

The short terrace of four houses on Beach Road built between 1901 and 1907 by an entrepreneur who had heard that the railway was coming to Happisburgh.

course extended westwards. His architectural plans and concept drawings survive, but the abandonment of the proposed railway and the onset of the First World War meant that the project never came to fruition: had this extension to the village been built it would have made a huge difference to the consequential history of Happisburgh!

A sketched architect's impression of the proposed development scheme at Happisburgh, designed and drawn by C.E. Mallows, 1909.

St Mary's

This period of expansion also saw the construction of one of the most architecturally significant buildings in the village, the Grade II*-listed house known as St Mary's, referred to by some as Happisburgh Manor. The house was designed in 1900 by architect Detmar Blow for Mrs Albemarle Cator, and is laid out in a butterfly, or X-shaped, plan, with two pairs of diagonal ranges emanating from a rectangular central range (NHER 14148). The design was heavily influenced by Ernest Gimson and he may have supervised and supplied the timber roof structure – several preliminary drawings by Gimson are at the Cheltenham Art Gallery.

It is an incredibly attractive house, constructed in the local vernacular manner using locally sourced materials – flint, pebbles, brick,

The impressive western façade of St Mary's, designed by Detmar Blow in 1900, showing the skilful use of flint, brick and thatch in the Arts and Crafts style.

thin tiles and thatch – an architectural approach firmly in keeping with the Arts and Crafts movement of the day. On the gable-ends of each of the diagonal ranges the words 'Ave Maria Stella Maris' – Hail, Mary, star of the sea – are picked out in ironwork, with one word on each gable. The house is surrounded by an oval wall, which encloses a formal garden to the rear, backed by a terrace with striking views across to the sea. The gardens are of importance in their own right, and are listed in English Heritage's National Parks and Gardens register.

Spread over three storeys, the ground floor focuses around the central room, with reception rooms radiating from it in each of the wings, while the first and second storeys are a maze of winding staircases, bedrooms, bathrooms and attics tucked under the eaves. All of the rooms have casement windows with stunning views of the sea and the village, many of their lintels are formed from layers of thin tiles, as are the surrounds of the many fireplaces to be found throughout the property.

St Mary's was commandeered for military use as officers' quarters during both of the world wars, and suffered major bomb damage in December 1941 when it received a direct hit. The house was restored and served as a country club and restaurant until 1987. It would seem that a lobby entrance was added to the house during this period, the front door having previously entered straight into the main room,

An aerial photograph of St Mary's in 1992, showing the butterfly plan and the gardens laid out around the house. (© Norfolk County Council; Photograph by D.A. Edwards: TG3831/A/GJV3)

The view looking north along Whimpwell Street from Millar's Pond in the early years of the 20th century. The forge is on the corner of Beach Lane and the newly constructed St Mary's is starkly highlighted against the sky to the extreme right of the frame.

presenting a view of the fireplace surmounted by a date and motto. The house again became a private residence in 1989, and in 2010 was bought by Amazing Retreats, who have extensively renovated the interior of the property as a high-end holiday let.

The long driveway to the house is flanked by stable-blocks, also by Blow and of the same period, now converted to residential use, and to the south is another Blow house – St Anne's – which again employs the same architectural styling and has an L-shaped plan (NHER 24941).

Henry Moore and Barbara Hepworth

In the early 1930s, a group of artists, including Barbara Hepworth, Henry Moore and Ben Nicholson, holidayed in Happisburgh, staying at the 18th-century Church Farm on the western edge of the village (NHER 43049). The group's first holiday was in 1930, when the party comprised Barbara Hepworth and her then husband John Skeaping, Henry Moore and his wife Irena, Hepworth's friends Douglas and Mary Jenkins, and painter Ivon Hitchens. The group spent a lot of time on the beach, where they picked up ironstone pebbles, on which

when carved and polished shone like bronze – several of Hepworth, Moore and Skeaping's subsequent sculptures were carved from this material.

While the holiday provided artistic inspiration, it did not help Hepworth and Skeaping's failing marriage. In the spring of 1931, Hepworth met Ben and Winifred Nicholson, and the two couples stuck up a friendship. When they holidayed in Happisburgh again in September 1931, Ben Nicholson joined the group, while his wife remained with their family in Cumbria. Skeaping, who had recently asked Hepworth for a divorce remained in London, but after a change of heart also came to Happisburgh, only to find that Hepworth had fallen in love with Nicholson. The couple eventually married in 1938, after both of them had left their respective spouses (Thornton 2009).

Hepworth wrote about Happisburgh in several of her letters, describing the scenery thus: 'the country is quite flat but for a little hill with a tall flint church and a lighthouse … the beach is a ribbon of pale sand as far as the eye can see.' She also wrote of the artists collecting ironstones from the beach and packing them up in crates to be transported back to London. It is

Henry Moore and friends on holiday at Happisburgh in Norfolk, 1931: (left to right) Ivon Hitchens, Irina Moore, Henry Moore, Barbara Hepworth, Ben Nicholson and Mary Jenkins, whose husband took the picture. (Reproduced by permission of the Henry Moore Foundation)

The view from Church Farm in the late 1920s, largely as it would have appeared to Henry Moore and Barbara Hepworth when they holidayed here in 1930 and 1931. (From the Neil Storey Archive)

clear that these two holidays in Happisburgh had profound professional and personal effects on all of the artists, Hepworth and Moore in particular, and that the memory of their time in the village continued to influence their work for years to come.

A Dissenting Voice

Of course, not everyone has been enamoured with their visit to Happisburgh. The Norfolk antiquary Walter Rye, in his 1885 book *A History of Norfolk*, recorded the following:

> 'The view from the cliffs is a fine one, and the sands are very firm and good for bathing, though there is, or was, only one machine. Some few houses let lodgings, and good accommodation can usually be had at the 'Hill House', which is a roomy and well-conducted inn, with a pretty bowling green' (Rye 1885, 245).

A positive enough start, but he continued:

> 'There are, however, certain objections to the place, which should be stated by an honest chronicler. There is only one little general shop; no meat is to be bought except at arbitrary and erratic intervals; the seven miles that divide the place from North Walsham, where are the nearest railway station and doctor, are over the vilest roads that I have ever had the hap to come across, chiefly consisting of sea beach; no newspaper or book has ever been seen in the village; everyone is expected to be in bed at nine; and dullness reigns supreme over the district. Cowper used to come here, and Cowper afterwards went mad, and I don't at all wonder at it. As a substitute for Spain or Chili, I may conscientiously recommend the place to absconding city accountants, for no one would ever dream of looking here for anybody' (Rye 1885, 245).

The vast numbers of holidaymakers who have and continue to flock to Happisburgh, many of them returning time after time, clearly show Walter Rye to be in the minority. Long may it continue!

Chapter 12

◇

Happisburgh at War

As a vulnerable coastal location, Happisburgh was garrisoned and heavily fortified during both the First and Second World Wars. During the First World War, the Rough Riders were stationed in the village. They were a cavalry division drawn from various parts of the country and photographs taken during the war show them training on Happisburgh beach. Many of the troops were billeted in private houses, and the recently completed St Mary's was requisitioned as an officers' mess. In order to protect against an enemy landing, trenches were dug along the clifftops and access to the beach was barred, although some local residents secured written permission from the Lieutenant Colonel of the forces stationed in the village allowing them access to the beach. The permission slips stated that the individuals were not to approach any of the defence works and they were not to go onto the beach between sunset and sunrise.

Fortunately, despite all of the preparations and troop placements, the only enemy action to directly touch the village was when a zeppelin dropped a bomb on Walcott Hall, killing two horses. Mr and Mrs George Gibbs and their family took shelter under the kitchen table during the raid.

The church contains two memorials to those who served in the armed forces during the First World War. The first of these is a carved marble tablet listing the names of those who lost their lives: Richard Grimmer, Norman Leeder, John Mason, William Miller, George Monsey, John Monsey, James Platford, Cubitt C. Siely, James Spanton and F. George Wiseman. The second memorial also lists these names, but more unusually also lists the names of the 83 other

This pair of rather poor quality photographs show the massed ranks of the Rough Riders drilling their horses on Happisburgh beach during the First World War.

One of the Rough Riders riding through the village.

A postcard showing a group of Officers billeted at St Mary's. The message on the back identifies (left to right) Capt. R H Love, Lieut. E Elliott, Lieut. G Wingate and Major C P Hines, who also sent the card. (From the Neil Storey Archive)

A postcard showing the collected Officers and NCOs, who the message on the reverse identifies as belonging to the Essex Regiment, in charge of Coastal Defences 1915–16. Sent by Major C P Hines. (From the Neil Storey Archive)

The memorial to the ten Happisburgh men who fell in the Great War.

men from the village who served in the war and returned safely.

World War Two
During the Second World War extensive coastal defences were installed at Happisburgh: the beach was mined and placed out of bounds, and high coils of barbed wire lined the clifftops. Numerous pillboxes were built to defend the coast, the first line of defence being on the clifftop itself, with a second line placed a few hundred metres inland. Road blocks comprising concrete blocks and iron posts which could be set in the road were readied for quick assembly.

The second memorial to the Great War, listing those who fell and those who survived.

Large numbers of troops were stationed in the village, and the army requisitioned several houses, including St Mary's, The Monastery (where the WRVS ran a canteen) and the Old Rectory. A gun battery was initially constructed at the end Beach Road, although this was later moved north beyond the church, and a radar station was built near to White's Farm.

Above left: *A Second World War pillbox on Beach Road. This is an unusual example, in that it is made from brick, not concrete, and appears to be circular.*

Above right: *Although a large number of Happisburgh's Second World War pillboxes survive, some of them have fallen victim to erosion. This example stood on the clifftops until the late 1960s, when it was undermined by the sea and fell onto the beach. Remarkably, it landed on its roof and remained intact.*

These two postcards show the view north along the beach from the top of the cliffs near Cart Gap. They were taken after the end of the Second World War, but before the construction of the sea defences in the late 1950s. In the foreground of this image are several of the concrete anti-tank cubes which would have blocked the route from the beach up onto the cliffs during the war. In the middle distance on the left-hand side of the frame the remains of a Second World War pillbox can be clearly seen. An alternative view of these same remains is offered by the second photograph, and both images clearly illustrate how some of the area's Second World War defences began to collapse shortly after the end of the war.

Happisburgh 4.7-Inch Coastal Battery

by James Albone (Historic Environment Service)
A World War Two coastal 4.7 inch gun battery was located on the clifftop to the northwest of Happisburgh village (NHER 18472). This site was constructed in late 1940 to replace a 6-inch battery originally located 1.3km to the south-east (NHER 32636). The earlier emergency battery had two gun houses with 6-inch guns and a two-storey observation post disguised as a holiday chalet. It had been located on the cliff edge and was instantly under threat from the rapidly eroding cliffs.

Whether or not the problem was exacerbated by the guns being fired is not clear. Aerial photographs show that the first site was disused and its replacement fully operational by July 1941. The 4.7-inch battery had two brick gun houses with flat concrete roofs. Typically, these were linked by underground magazines and stores. Both of the gun houses had pitched thatched roofs to camouflage them as haystacks. The two-storey battery observation post to the south-east

of the gun houses was camouflaged as a civilian building.

The two searchlights for the battery were located some 200m south-east and 330m north-west of the gun houses. Both were recessed into the clifftop with a sunken concrete track leading to the cliff edge. Wooden huts associated with the site were concealed along hedgerows.

The core of the battery was protected by a rectangular barbed wire enclosure, divided into three sections. The landward side of this was protected by a Type 22 pillbox and at least one spigot mortar emplacement. The site was further surrounded by a polygonal barbed wire enclosure that included the searchlight positions, and was protected by three Type 27 pillboxes and other gun emplacements. The defences surrounding the battery linked in to the continuous line of barbed wire and other anti-invasion defences along the cliffs and beach. The Happisburgh battery was transferred to Home Guard control in 1943 and reduced to a 'care and maintenance' status. With the exception of a site

A 1992 aerial photograph of the remains of the Happisburgh 4.7-Inch Coastal Battery, one of the best preserved examples of its type in the county. (© Norfolk County Council; Photograph taken by D.A. Edwards: TG3731/F/GJV1)

at West Caister, the 4.7-inch Happisburgh battery is the best preserved of all the coastal batteries in Norfolk. Both of the gun houses survive with their underground magazines, though they are largely inaccessible. To the rear of the gun houses are two extant pillboxes, a common Type 22 and a more rare Type 27.

Happisburgh Chain Home Low radar station

by James Albone (Historic Environment Service)
Happisburgh Chain Home Low radar station and associated defences are visible on World War Two and later aerial photographs. The earliest aerial photographs showing the radar station date from August 1940 and show the first incarnation of the radar site – Happisburgh I – which consisted of two groups of buildings. The Happisburgh II radar station, constructed in 1942, incorporated these two areas, but also included a substantial mast and associated buildings. The only World War Two aerial photographs to show the whole of the

An aerial photograph of the site of Happisburgh radar station, taken by the RAF in July 1946. Although many of the wartime defences had been removed by this time, it is still possible to see many of the buildings associated with the radar station including the mast. Although the image is looking straight down onto the mast, in the centre of the frame, the low angle of sunlight causes it to cast a long shadow across the fields. (© Crown Copyright: TG33/TG3630/B)

Happisburgh II site date from 1943, at that time the majority of the site was surrounded by a polygonal barbed wire enclosure measuring approximately 400m by 240m. Several weapons pits and gun emplacements were present around this perimeter. A curving barbed wire defence extended from the north side of the main area and included two weapons pits or gun emplacements and a pillbox, which still survives (NHER 32633).

Details of the buildings at the radar site are not clearly visible on the 1943 aerial photographs, however the buildings are visible on aerial photographs dating from 1946 to 1955. Most buildings were located at the roadside site, included a large building with protective earth banks on its north side. Part of this building is still extant, and is now used as an agricultural store. A second building surrounded by earth banks and a blast wall was located further to the north – it is possible that this was the transmitter/receiver building from the Happisburgh I site. To the north and west of this building were three blast wall-protected nissen huts.

The 54m (180ft) high Happisburgh II aerial mast was located to the north-east of Happisburgh I, with a second low level aerial positioned 30m to its north. The operations block was positioned between these two aerials, and this building and the concrete bases of the mast survive. An associated anti aircraft gun battery (NHER 38792) was located immediately to the north of the radar station.

Members of the Happisburgh Heritage Group undertaking an historic building survey at the site of the former Happisburgh Radar Station in November 2010.

149

The Home Guard and Civil Defence

The Happisburgh Section of the Home Guard, originally called the Local Defence Volunteers, consisted of one lieutenant, three sergeants, three corporals, seven lance corporals and 58 privates. Their primary role was to defend the village in the event of invasion. They met weekly on Sunday mornings when practice included parade ground and battle drill, small arms firing and camouflage.

For civil defence purposes Norfolk was divided into small areas. The Bacton Group consisted of the parishes of Bacton, East Ruston, Happisburgh, Ridlington, Walcott and Witton. Happisburgh had twelve Wardens, six Fire Fighters, 42 Fire Watchers, 28 Auxiliary Fire Watchers and the Head Warden of the Bacton Group. One of the responsibilities of Civil Defence was to arrange for emergency rations of biscuits, beef, sugar, soup, milk, margarine and tea to be stored in the village. These were kept at Fairview, The Forge and Manor Farm. In 1939, members of Civil Defence issued respirators to all in the village – 504 altogether.

Extracts from the Civil Defence Logbook

The Old Rectory was destroyed by bombs on Sunday 27 October 1940. A stick of six bombs was dropped, two falling in the churchyard. The remains of the stable block and coach house of the Old Rectory have since been incorporated into The Lodge. Windows were blown out in the church and had to be shuttered. The Civil Defence logbook recorded the following account of the raid:

'27 October 1940, 18:04hrs: First Enemy Air Raid on Happisburgh – no warning received from Control. Fighter bombers attempted to bomb Norwich, but were intercepted and driven off by British fighters. One Enemy plane ... dropped three sticks of bombs including five on Church Farm buildings, four by the road, three in Churchyard (ricochet near porch), one or two on Old Rectory and portion demolished, one in field near old Lifeboat House. Two Casualties

This photograph taken shortly after the end of the war shows the bomb-damaged church with boarded up windows. The building in the foreground is all that remained of the Old Rectory, much of which was so damaged in the raid that it had to be pulled down.

The Old Rectory as it appeared before being irreparably damaged in the 1940 air raid. (From the Neil Storey Archive)

(minor), both Military. One horse killed at Church Farm. Damage: Church – all windows on south side completely blown out, all others badly damaged. Old Rectory – partly demolished. Manor House – back roof stripped. Fairview – north and west windows blown out. Church Cottage and Albion Cottage – north and east windows out, chimney stack lifted, roofs damaged, telephone post cut through. Danegate – front windows out.'

Several other incidents are also recorded in the Civil Defence logbook:

'6 May 1941, 00:20hrs: Four HEs [High Explosives] exploded near Coastguard Station ... Extensive damage to Coastguard Cottages, Cliff Houses and others – about 42 premises affected. ... One slight casualty to soldier at St Mary's. Incident reported before sound of explosion reached Control at North Walsham.'

'16 October 1941, 05:15hrs: British fighter crashed in sea In flames off Hasbro' Gap about

100yrds out. Reported immediately. ... Cromer Lifeboat picked up one dead airman; the other washed ashore Oct. 19th.'

'18 December 1941, 08.13hrs: Enemy plane, believed Messerschmitt, dropped two HEs (500kg). One exploded at St Mary's, the other 150yds away in field near Beach Lane. Casualties: All Military – two dead, four stretcher cases, one serious; five or six slight cuts by flying glass. Damage: Back portion of St Mary's ... and one wing demolished. Approx. 50 other dwellings damaged.'

'4 August 1943, 00:27hrs: One Enemy Raider dropped three containers of AP bombs in field and meadows around Old Mill Farm, Lower Hasbro' and two 50kg HEs near Lessingham School. (92 anti-personnel bombs dropped; 51 unexploded. Search by 5 police and 4 wardens.'

'5 August 1944, 08.55hrs: USAAF Liberator bomber crashed but did not catch fire. All crew baled out.'

Extracts from the Joel family diaries

The Joel family – Mr and Mrs Joel and their four sons – lived in a two-storey timber house at Cart

Gap from 1936 and 1945. Several members of the family kept wartime diaries, extracts from which record a number of exchanges in the ongoing conflict:

17 February 1941: 'Greatest excitement of my life watching two Spitfires firing at a Hun plane. It disappeared in the clouds over the sea, but was firing and being fired at all the time. Two young sergeant pilots in the Spitfires brought it down in the sea. A destroyer went towards the scene.'

20 February 1941: 'Daddy cycling to collect the twins got machine gunned by a Hun [aircraft]. He fell off his bike into the hedge. Other people also fired at. The Hun passed over the house firing all the time and disappeared in mist over the sea.'

13 March 1941: 'A terrific row at midnight, bombing, etc. A lovely ship in flames out to sea. We watched her exploding and sinking.'

23 July 1941: 'A young officer is blown up (and killed) by a mine at the dunes.'

Mrs Joel was not the only member of the family to record wartime actions in her diary; her son, David, also recorded the following incidents:

10 December 1941: 'A Dornier 215 [had] bombed a ship which was no more than 800 yards out. …

The Dornier dropped one bomb near to the last ship of a small convoy of two tugs, each towing a barge, and two merchant ships.'

18 December 1941: 'St Mary's, Happisburgh, was bombed at 8:10 this morning. There have been several casualties. The North Wing was hit by a heavy bomb'.

German War Graves

There are a large number of burials recorded in the parish registers for unknown sailors and airmen whose bodies were washed up on the Happisburgh coast during the two World Wars. The parish burial register contains three entries for the burials of German combatants whose bodies were washed ashore in October 1939: Lieutenant Heinz Schlicht, a German naval officer, Lieutenant Fritz Meyer a German air officer, and a Sergeant Wessels, a German airman. All three men were buried in Happisburgh churchyard with full military honours on 2 November 1939, and photographs record the three coffins draped with German flags and a volley of rifle shots being fired at the graveside (Mee 1940, 163).

The body of a fourth German, this time of an unidentified airman, was washed ashore the

A photograph of the funerals of the German airmen whose bodies had been washed ashore in Happisburgh.

following autumn and buried in the churchyard on 30 October 1940. These four German burials remained in the churchyard until 18 January 1963, when the remains of the four individuals were exhumed and relocated to the German Military Cemetery at Cannock Chase near Wolverhampton.

Peacetime

Despite the civilian and military casualties which occurred in and around the village during the Second World War, only eight Happisburgh men lost their lives in the conflict. They are commemorated on a plaque mounted on the wall of the church: A. Batchelor, R.A. Boyce, J.D. Clarke, B.B. Dennis, E.W. Grimmer, C.G. Harvey, C.W. Harvey and C.J. Pardon.

The final entry in the Operations Record Book of the Happisburgh radar station recorded the feelings of the commanding officer on the declaration of peace: 'In this rather remote corner of England the reaction was necessarily restrained, but due celebration was affected

The memorial to the eight Happisburgh men who died on active service during the Second World War.

within the capacity of the local hostelry, who quickly capitulated until the siege, and finally succumbed under the flurry of raised arms (and elbows). ... Happisburgh Final Scoreboard: Destroyed 37, Probables 13, Damaged 7. We regret we had not the opportunity to make it an even total. In the hour of final victory, opportunity was taken by all ranks to tender our thanks to HIM who has guided and sustained us throughout the dark periods.'

Looking Forward

Happisburgh is a truly remarkable place, with a story which spans the full range of human history, from the earliest human ancestors until the present day. In putting together this book, we have drawn together a number of disparate sources and drawn on several decades of research to showcase some of the historical and archaeological highlights of the Happisburgh story, and remind people that there is more to Happisburgh than sensationalist stories about coastal erosion. We have, of course, only scratched the surface.

There is enormous scope for future research into the history of Happisburgh, and each of the subjects touched on here could easily be expanded into a book of its own. The Norfolk Record Office contains a vast archive relating to the parish, including several historic maps (barely touched on here) and a large number of wills, probate inventories, sale particulars and other documents. Similarly, the potential for further significant archaeological discoveries to be made in the parish is very high. Materials relating to early human occupation are likely to continue to appear from beneath the beach, and, now that readers are familiar with the flint handaxes discovered to date, they are encouraged to be vigilant when they are on the beach. Similarly, as the cliffs continue to erode, further archaeological artefacts from more recent, but still relatively ancient, periods might well be revealed. Again, vigilance and timely reporting of discoveries are the key.

During the autumn of 2010, a group of individuals who had become involved with the Coastal Heritage Project element of the North Norfolk District Pathfinder decided that they wanted to form the Happisburgh Heritage Group. A constitution for the group was drawn up and the group adopted the following stated aims:

- to procure, develop and maintain an archive of photographs, documents, audio and video recordings, artefacts and other materials relating to Happisburgh's heritage, and an index of such material held by other organisations and individuals;
- to pursue original research into Happisburgh's heritage
- to gather oral histories;
- to organise and carry out site visits, surveys and archaeological activities within and outside the area;
- to act as a resource for material and information for schools, libraries, mass media, museums, etc.;
- to hold meetings, lectures and temporary and/or permanent exhibitions;
- to produce papers, reports, booklets and other literature; and
- to publish appropriate material on the Happisburgh Village website.

In order to help the new group achieve its aims, the Coastal Heritage Project was able to provide a series of training sessions focussed on different research techniques and also an equipment grant, to cover the costs of computing, recording and surveying equipment.

To date, the group have begun to create an archive of historic images of the parish, for which further contributions are invited; they are undertaking a series of oral history interviews, recording people's memories of life in the village; they are conducting a survey of the gravestones in the churchyard, recording the inscriptions while they are still legible; and they have begun recording the parish's surviving Second World War buildings, beginning with the radar station and the gun battery. Anyone who is interested in joining the Happisburgh Heritage Group should visit their page on the village website: www.happisburgh.org/heritage.

At the time of writing, in 2011, the landscape of Happisburgh is again about to change very dramatically, although this time as a result of the North Norfolk Pathfinder Project and not the effects of erosion. Having bought many of the threatened houses on Beach Road, North Norfolk District Council intend to demolish them to create a greatly enhanced clifftop area, complete with a new car park and beach access ramp. The Happisburgh Heritage Group intend to make sure that these changes are documented for future generations, today's present being tomorrow's history.

Bibliography

Primary sources, such as parish registers, wills and probate inventories referred to in the text are all held by the Norfolk Record Office – indicated by an NRO prefix – unless otherwise stated.
All of the archaeological records referred to are held by the Norfolk Historic Environment Record – indicated by an NHER prefix – unless otherwise stated

Albone, J., Massey, S. and Temlett, S. 2007. *The Archaeology of Norfolk's Coastal Zone: Results of the National Mapping Programme.* English Heritage Project Report No. 2913.

Alecto. 2002. *The Digital Domesday Book.* CD ROM. Hampshire.

Arnold, C. and Wardle, D. 1981. 'Early Medieval Settlement Patterns in England', *Medieval Archaeology* 25, 145–9.

Ashton, N., Parfitt, S.A., Lewis, S.G., Coope, G.R. and Larkin, N. 2008. 'Happisburgh Site 1 (TG388307)' in Candy, I., Lee, J.R., and Harrison, A.M. (eds) *The Quaternary of Northern East Anglia: Field Guide.* Edinburgh. pp.151–6.

Ashwin, T. 2005a. 'Norfolk's First Farmers: Early Neolithic Norfolk (*c.*4000–3000 BC)' in Ashwin, T. and Davison, A. (eds) *An Historical Atlas of Norfolk.* Third edition. Chichester. pp.17–18.

Ashwin, T. 2005b. 'Late Neolithic and Early Bronze-Age Norfolk (*c.*3000–1700 BC)' in Ashwin, T. and Davison, A. (eds) *An Historical Atlas of Norfolk.* Third edition. Chichester. pp.19–20.

Ashwin, T. 2005c. 'Later Bronze-Age Norfolk (*c.*1700–700 BC)' in Ashwin, T. and Davison, A. (eds) *An Historical Atlas of Norfolk.* Third edition. Chichester. pp.21–2.

Banyer, M. and Clark, M. 2003. 'Happisburgh Signal Box – another First!', *M&GN Circle Bulletin* 505, 14–15.

Caraman, P. (trans.). 1951. *John Gerard: The Autobiography of an Elizabethan.* London.

Cattermole, P. 1990. *Church Bells and Bell-Ringing: A Norfolk Profile.* Woodbridge.

Cattermole, P. 2007a. 'The Benedictine Monastery' in Cattermole, P. (ed.) *Wymondham Abbey.* Wymondham. pp.39–63.

Cattermole, P. 2007b. 'Outlying Estates' in Cattermole, P. (ed.) *Wymondham Abbey.* Wymondham. pp.58–9.

Darby, H. 1971. *The Domesday Geography of Eastern England.* Second edition. Cambridge.

Darvill, T. 1987. *Prehistoric Britain.* London.

Defoe, D. 1949 [1724]. *Tour Through the Eastern Counties.* East Anglian Magazine.

Gurney, D. 2005. 'Roman Norfolk (*c.*AD 43–410)' in Ashwin, T. and Davison, A. (eds) *An Historical Atlas of Norfolk.* Third edition. Chichester. pp.28–9.

Hoggett, R. 2010. *The Archaeology of the East Anglian Conversion.* Woodbridge.

Hutcheson, N. 2005. 'The End of Prehistory: Gold, Silver, Boudica and the Romans' in Ashwin, T. and Davison, A. (eds) *An Historical Atlas of Norfolk.* Third edition. Chichester. pp.26–7.

Hutcheson, N. and Ashwin, T. 2005. 'Iron-Age Norfolk (*c.*700 BC–AC 43)' in Ashwin, T. and Davison, A. (eds) *An Historical Atlas of Norfolk.* Third edition. Chichester. pp.23–5.

Mee, A. 1940. *The King's England: Norfolk.* London.

Page, W. (ed.) 1906. *The Victoria History of the County of Norfolk*. Volume 2. Edinburgh.

Parfitt, S. 2008. 'Pakefield Cliffs: Archaeology and Palaeoenvironment of the Cromer Forest-bed Formation' in Candy, I., Lee, J.R., and Harrison, A.M. (eds) *The Quaternary of Northern East Anglia: Field Guide*. Edinburgh. pp.130–6.

Parfitt, S.A., Ashton, N.M., Lewis, S.G., *et al.* 2010. 'Early Pleistocene human occupation at the edge of the boreal zone in northwest Europe', *Nature* 466, 229–33.

Penn, K. 2005. 'Early Saxon Settlement (*c.* AD 410–650)' in Ashwin, T. and Davison, A. (eds) *An Historical Atlas of Norfolk*. Third edition. Chichester. pp.30–1.

Pestell, T. 1993. *Archaeological Excavations on the Foreshore of Eccles Beach, Norfolk. A Second Interim Report*. Unpublished archaeological report.

Pevsner, N. and Wilson, B. 1997. *Norfolk I: Norwich and North-East*. London.

Preece, R.C. and Parfitt, S.A. 2008. 'The Cromer Forest-bed Formation: some recent developments relating to early human occupation and lowland glaciation' in Candy, I., Lee, J.R., and Harrison, A.M. (eds) *The Quaternary of Northern East Anglia: Field Guide*. Edinburgh. pp.60–83.

Raithby, J. (ed.) 1819. *Statutes of the Realm, Volume 5: 1628–80*. London:

Reynolds, A. 1999. *Later Anglo-Saxon England*. Stroud.

Rippon, S. 2008. *Beyond the Medieval Village*. Oxford.

Robins, P., Wymer, J.J. and Parfitt, S.A. 2009. 'Handaxe finds on the Norfolk Beaches', *Norfolk Archaeology* 45(iii), 412–15.

Roffe, D. 2000. *Domesday: The Inquest and the Book*. Oxford.

Rye. W. 1885. *A History of Norfolk*. London.

Sandred, K.I., Cornford, B., Lindstrom, B. and Rutledge, P. 1996. *The Place-names of Norfolk. Part Two: The Hundreds of East and West Flegg, Happing and Tunstead*. Nottingham.

Shopland, A. 2007. 'Founders and Benefactors' in Cattermole, P. (ed.) *Wymondham Abbey*. Wymondham. pp.17–29.

Spiller, R.E. 1927. 'A New Biographical Source for William Cowper', *PMLA* 42(4), pp.946–62.

Stoker, B. 1907. *Personal Reminiscences of Henry Irving*. London.

Storey, N. 2009. *The Lost Coast of Norfolk*. Stroud.

Stringer, C. 2006. *Homo Britannicus*. London.

Thornton, N. 2009. *Moore Hepworth Nicholson: A nest of gentle artists in the 1930s*. Norwich.

Tikus, A. 2003. *The Ship-wrecks off North Norfolk*. West Walton.

Tikus, A. 2004. *The Ship-wrecks off North East Norfolk*. West Walton.

Tipper, J. 2004. *The Grubenhaus in Anglo-Saxon England*. Yedingham.

Wacher, J. 1998. *Roman Britain*. Stroud.

Williamson, T. 1993. *The Origins of Norfolk*. Manchester.

Wilson, D.R. 2000. *Air Photo Interpretation for Archaeologists*. Stroud.

White, W. 1836. *History, Gazetteer and Directory of Norfolk*. Sheffield.

Williams, J. 1946. *Diocese of Norwich. Bishop Redman's Visitation, 1597. Presentations in the Archdeaconries of Norwich, Norfolk, and Suffolk.*. Norwich.

Wymer, J. 2005a. 'Occupation Before the Last Glaciation: The Palaeolithic Period' ' in Ashwin, T. and Davison, A. (eds) *An Historical Atlas of Norfolk*. Third edition. Chichester. pp.13–14.

Wymer, J. 2005b. 'Late Glacial and Mesolithic Hunters (c.10,000–4000 BC)' in Ashwin, T. and Davison, A. (eds) *An Historical Atlas of Norfolk*. Third edition. Chichester. pp.15–16.

Wymer, J. and Robins, P. 2006. 'Happisburgh and Pakefield: The Earliest Britons', *Current Archaeology* 201, 458–67.

Subscribers

Jennifer Ablett, briefly of Lantern Lane, Happisburgh

Rosalyn Aitken (née Siely), Amersham, Bucks

Anita J. Allison, Happisburgh

Brian Alton, Sheringham, Norfolk

Helena Ancell, Happisburgh, Norfolk

Mrs Sylvia Andrews, Walcott, Norfolk

Catherine Andrews (née Palfrey, Happisburgh)

D. J. M. Armstrong, Ridlington, Norfolk

David Bacon, Happisburgh, Norfolk

Michael and Margaret Badcock, Sawston, Cambridge

Frances and John Bailey, Happisburgh

Pat and Bill Bailey, Whimpwell Green, Norfolk

Mrs L. Balls, Happisburgh

K. and D. Banthorpe, Happisburgh, Norfolk

Eric and Doris Bates, Happisburgh, Norfolk

Chris and Elaine Batt, Happisburgh

Mr and Mrs T. Beane, Happisburgh, Norfolk

Mr and Mrs M. Beane (née Watling), Happisburgh

Mr and Mrs T. Beeby

Glenn and Joanna Berry, Happisburgh

Wendy Boddington, Happisburgh Common

J. and E. Bowler, Smallburgh, Norfolk

Helen Bowles, grew up in Happisburgh

Roger Brighton, 38-50 Light House, Walcott

Allan and Pauline Brown, Bovingdon, Hertfordshire

Margaret, John, Jayne Buckingham, Happisburgh, Norfolk

Stephen and Denise Burke, Happisburgh

Jan Burley, Happisburgh

Michael and Betty Burn, Happisburgh

Christine M. Butler (née Faulke), Horsford

D. Chadwick, Yorkshire

Joseph and Benjamin Chant of Amersham and Happisburgh

Peter and Tina Chant of Amersham and Happisburgh

Poppy and Lola Chant of Breaston and Happisburgh

Terry Charman, Chalton, Bedfordshire

Simon (Son of Eileen and Ivor) and Elizabeth Clarke, Benest, France

Jeremy (Son of Eileen and Ivor) and Anne Clarke, Johannesburg, South Africa

Andrew (Son of Eileen and Ivor) and Gill Clarke, Sheringham, Norfolk

Mr C. Clarke, Norwich (born in Happisburgh)

The Clarke family, Seashell

The Colliers, Market Harborough, Leics

Alice and Claude Cook, Manor Cottage, Happisburgh, Norfolk

The Coopers and Lightfoots, Happy Holidays

Mrs Joy Cuddington, Happisburgh

Cedric and Gill Cullingford

Ivy Cumbers (née Winn), Norwich

Mr and Mrs Denman, South Norwood Hill, London

Peter B. Dennis, Walcott, Norfolk

Philip W. Dennis, Norwich

Jean and Peter Dickinson, Happisburgh, Norfolk

Jill Dixon, Norwich, Norfolk

Liz Dixon and Robert Payne, Happisburgh, Norfolk

Philip Doughty, Grantham, Lincolnshire

Chris and Chris Dye, Happisburgh

E13 Manor Caravan Park 1970s-1980s

William Easton, Norwich, Norfolk

Jeanette Ellis, Eccles-on-Sea, Norfolk

Shirley Everett, Blakeney, Norfolk

Bethan Falkowska, London, England

The Hodder family

G. and D. Farmer, Happisburgh

John and Chris Fenby

Ron Fiske, Morningthorpe

Carole and Robert Fleming, Happisburgh

C. and J. Flint, St Neots, Cambridgeshire

Barbara M. Forder, Happisburgh, Norfolk

Amanda G. Forder, Happisburgh, Norfolk

Jason M. Francis, The Pink House, Happisburgh

James Garrett-Pegge, Happisburgh

Mr and Mrs P. Gee, Haslemere, Surrey

Diane and John Gibbons, Harleston

Joyce and Tony Gibson, High Kelling, Norfolk

Richard and Ruth Gilbert, Long Eaton, Derbyshire

Robert and Louise Gilbert, Rainford, Merseyside

Jill and David Gilbert, Attenborough, Nottingham

Janet Gilmour, Cart Gap, Norfolk

Maurene Gilson, Happisburgh

Tim Gimmer, Happisburgh

Brian Golder, Nuneaton, Warwickshire

Paul J. Goodman, Happisburgh

The Goodwille Family, Doggetts Lane, Cart Gap, Happisburgh

Ian Gotts, South Wootton, Norfolk

J. Gotts, Happisburgh, Norfolk

C. E. Grady, Little Melton, Norfolk

Garry and Kay Greatbanks

Mr and Mrs C. J. Greavner, Happisburgh, Norfolk

Chris Green, Happisburgh, Norfolk

Gwen and Russell Green, spent many happy holidays in Happisburgh

Marion Green, Wroxham, Norfolk
Bill and Carole Greeno, The Old Post Office,
    Happisburgh, Norfolk
Sarah Greenwood (née Dobson), Yorkshire
Mrs Dorothy Gregory, Ampthill, Beds
Margaret and Spencer Greystrong, Colchester
Bethany and Daisy Hale
Geoffrey Hales
Mr J. A. Hall, Happisburgh, Norfolk
David Hardy, Happisburgh
P. C. Harley, Norwich, Norfolk
Samantha Harrison, North Walsham, Norfolk
Mr D. Hart, New Zealand
Jackie Hart (née Marshall)
Frank Harvey, Ipswich
The Harveys
J. M. Hatt, Happisburgh, Norfolk
Pam and Mike Hatton, Heald Green, Cheshire
Nora Hawksworth (née Siely), Northrepps
Roger Haywood, Happisburgh
R and M. Henderson, Lessingham
Elizabeth Hepburn (née Elvin), Ipswich,
    former resident of Church Farm, Happisburgh
Eddie and Mary Higgins, Cheltenham,
    Gloucestershire
Historic Environment Service, Norfolk County
    Council
Dr Peter G. Hoare, Ely, Cambridgeshire
Carl and Wendy Hoggett
Margaret Jane House
Robert C. Howe, Aldham, Suffolk
Barbara J. Howe, Happisburgh, Norfolk
Maria Howe-Li-Rocchi, Gt Ellingham
William Hoyland, Happisburgh
Christopher Joel, ex Happisburgh
Mrs M. Johns (née Clarke), Thorpe St Andrew,
    Norwich
Sue Jones (née Austerberry), Welshpool, Powys
J. A. Kelly, Norwich, Norfolk
Sharon Kelly, Happisburgh
Duncan E. Kirrage, Beane, Happisburgh, Norfolk
Sue Kirrage, Happisburgh, Norfolk
Dr Robert Knee, North Walsham, Norfolk
Mr Alan J. Knight
A. Konury
Ian and Vi La Riviere, Park Street, St Albans, Herts
John H. La Riviere, Park Street, St Albans, Herts
Nigel Larkin
C. Larter, Beach Road
Joan M. Larter, Happisburgh, Norfolk
Derek Larter, Caistor St Edmunds, Norfolk
Gilbert E. Larter, Happisburgh, Norfolk
Daisy and Felix Last, Happisburgh
John and Anne Lawrence, Guildford, Surrey
Carole and Neville Lee
Peter M. Liell, Eccles, Norfolk
 Lin and Jim, Yeoman Barn, Grubb Street
Joe and Carolina Li-Rocchi, Heathersett

Peter R. Livermore
Peter, Sybil, Rachel Longley, Ludham, Norfolk
Mrs Ann Mancini, White Horse Common,
    North Walsham
Mrs P. Marsh, North Walsham
John and Carol Marshall, Happisburgh, Norfolk
Peter and Melanie Martin, Happisburgh, Norfolk
Herbert and Violet Mason, formerly of Mill Cottage,
    Happisburgh
Mrs M. Mason, Happisburgh
Ellen C. McDonald, Happisburgh, Norfolk
Hannah McDonald, Eccles-on-Sea
Mellows Brown & Co. Ltd, Hertfordshire
Lin and Dave Mole
John Monson, Ridlington, Norfolk
Jonathan Morris, Happisburgh
Margaret W. Muckersie, Happisburgh, Norfolk
Chris and Urs Mumenthaler
Paul and Rosemary Munday, Happisburgh, Norfolk
Peter and June Neale, Denver, Norfolk
E. Mary Oliver, Happisburgh, Norfolk
Ruth Oppelt (née Dobson), WA, USA
Catherine Osborne, Edingthorpe, Norfolk
Raffe Oxenden, Bacton, Norfolk
Carol Palfrey, Happisburgh
Pamela Parker (Owned 'Magnolia', Blacksmith
    Lane, Happisburgh), Leicester
The Parrys, Whimpwell House, Happisburgh
Lesley and Dilip Patel
Margaret Pearce, Eaton, Norwich
Mary Pegge, Chesham, Bucks
Keith Pittman, Diss
Andrew M. Plumb, Cambourne, Cambridge
David F. Plumb, Comberton, Cambridge
Alexandra Potter, Fradley Junction
Wendy Potter, Nuneaton, Warwickshire
Daphne Pritchard, Neatishead, Norfolk
Mr and Mrs Pugh, Pump Hill, Happisburgh
The Rhodes Family
Robert and Hazel Richardson (Walcott),
Steven Richter, grew up in Happisburgh
Rita and Mike, The Little Barn, Happisburgh
Kirsty J. Ritchie, Happisburgh, Norfolk
Sandra J. Ritchie, Happisburgh, Norfolk
Janet Rivett, Happisburgh, Norfolk
Carol and Keith Rogers, spent their honeymoon in
    Happisburgh
Shirley Rowan, Chesham, Bucks
Judith Rushmer (née Pestell), Smallburgh
Ray and Margaret Sanders, Happisburgh
Martin J. Sangster, Bacton, Norfolk
Seymour Family, Grays, Essex
Robyn Sheppard, 1 School Common Cottages,
    Happisburgh
David Siely
Syd Siely
George Siely
June Simmonds, Happisburgh

Antony G. Smith
Rita and Geoffrey Smith, enjoyed holidaying in
    Happisburgh
Francine Smith, Harrow, Middx
Kathryn and Paul Spark, Sawston, Cambridge
J. Stacey, Hemel Hempstead, Herts
Julian, Liz, Naomi and Oliver Stock
Ann Stockham, Mundesley, Norfolk
Douglas W. Stott, Ruskington, Lincolnshire
Sue Swaffield, Cambridge
The Swallow family (Hushey/Ridlington)
Mrs H. Swan, New Zealand
Andrew, Beverley, Joshua and Samuel Taylor,
    New Ash Green, Longfield, Kent
Ralph and Margaret Taylor, London, SE9
Fred Thompsett, Patcham, Sussex
P. G. and J. A. Thompson, Happisburgh
Sq. Ldr. George J. Thwaites MBE, RAF RTD
Ann Treloar (née Makepeace)
Patrick and Joy Tubby, Acle, Norfolk
Ray and Toni Tubby, Acle, Norfolk
Jessie Turland, Chilwell, Nottingham
Iris and Rod Voegeli, Norwich
Louise and Simon Wain, Chilwell, Nottingham
Wallace Family, Grays, Essex
Klaus Wallmach and Ulrike Kerner, Germany
Janet and Simon Ward, Hazlemere, Bucks
Clifford Watling, Happisburgh, Norfolk
Peter and Sharon Watling, Happisburgh, Norfolk

Sue and Jim Webster, Happisburgh, Norfolk
Barbara E. Weddall, Happisburgh, Norfolk
Wegg family of Happisburgh
E. H. Wenn (Happisburgh) Ltd
Linda and Michael Westall, Langtree, Devon
Mr Mark White and Diana White, Norwich, Norfolk
Jim and Mel Whiteside, Happisburgh
Simon and Pat Whiteside, Pullham St. Mary
Mr and Mrs Whitlock, Happisburgh, Norfolk
Enda M. Whitwood, Happisburgh, Norfolk
Alan and Margaret Whitwood, Happisburgh
Robert Whitwood, Happisburgh
George and Josie Whitworth, Eccles-on-Sea
David Wightman, Stamford, Lincs
Lorraine and Graham Wilkes, Moraira, Spain
Ray and Sue Wilks, Langley Upper Green, Essex
Mrs Elisabeth Wilson (née Payne, grandparents and
    parents owned 'The Monastery', Happisburgh
    from 1952-2006)
Val and John Winter
Ann Wood (née Gilmour), Cart Gap, Norfolk
Chris and Margot Wright, Redbourn
Mark R. Wright, Happisburgh, Norfolk
Daren B. Wright, Happisburgh, Norfolk
Lisa K. Wright, Happisburgh, Norfolk
Karen Wright (née Beane)
Diana Wrightson and Jill Morris, Happisburgh
Maureen L. Yaxley, Coltishall, Norfolk
Peter Young, Happisburgh